More praise for Tom Perrotta's *Bad Haircut* . . .

"MOVING . . . looks past the era's celebrated kitsch to still-relevant social and cultural issues and the timeless mysteries of growing up . . . A convincing portrait of a time of life, illuminating all the profound cruelty and tenderness of adolescence." —*Publishers Weekly*

"TOM PERROTTA HAS IT RIGHT—our much-divided youth, the big mysteries that come with body hair and fake IDs, the terror and delights that are our growing up." —Lee K. Abbott, author of *Living After Midnight* and *Dreams of Distant Lives*

"ONE OF THOSE CRAZY BOOKS ABOUT GROWING UP that makes us laugh and cry at once." —Bret Lott, author of *Jewel* and *Reed's Beach*

"BEAUTIFULLY RESTRAINED WRITING and [a] gift for nosing out small absurdities." —*Washington Post*

"DISTINGUISHED BY ITS USE OF CLEVER HUMOR and quiet metaphor, Perrotta's writing is vivid but unobtrusive; the stories offer the reader a clear window on an era." —*Miami Herald*

"SO SHARP AND SURE in its depiction of growing up . . . Because this set of stories, like those of J. D. Salinger, are so based in the kind of truth that spans generations, no reference to a particular decade is needed." —*Hartford Courant*

"AS SUBTLE AS STORIES BY RAYMOND CARVER . . . so much fun to read . . . Buddy will touch your heart." —*New Britain* (CT) *Herald*

*continued on next page* . . .

# BAD HAIRCUT

## Stories of the Seventies

## TOM PERROTTA

*Rank.*
*I hope you read this.*
*Stories from Harwood, N.J.*
*Our youth!*

*RM*

The characters and events in this book are fictitious. Any similarity to actual persons, living or dead, is coincidental and not intended by the author.

"The Wiener Man" first appeared in *Columbia Magazine;* "Forgiveness" in *Crazyhorse;* "Wild Kingdom" in *The Gettysburg Review.*

BAD HAIRCUT

A Berkley Book / published by arrangement with
Bridge Works Publishing

PRINTING HISTORY
Bridge Works Publishing edition published 1994
Berkley edition / October 1995

ISBN: 0-425-14942-0

BERKLEY®
Berkley Books are published by The Berkley Publishing Group,
200 Madison Avenue, New York, New York 10016.
BERKLEY and the "B" design
are trademarks belonging to Berkley Publishing Corporation.

PRINTED IN THE UNITED STATES OF AMERICA

10  9  8  7  6  5  4  3  2  1

# Contents

## For Mary

The author would like to thank the following people for their help and support: James Linville, Kimberly Witherspoon, Alexandra Shelley, Barbara and Warren Phillips, Lee K. Abbott, and Joe Gordon. Special thanks, of course, to Joe and Sue Perrotta, and to Mary Granfield.

# Bad Haircut

*Tom Perrotta*

# The Wiener Man

**M**y mother was a den mother, but she wasn't fanatical about it. Unlike Mrs. Kerner—the scoutmaster's wife and leader of our rival den—she didn't own an official uniform, nor did she attempt to educate us in the finer points of scouting, stuff like knot-tying, fire-building, and secret handshakes. She considered herself a glorified babysitter and pretty much let us do as we pleased at our meetings, just as long as we amused ourselves and kept out of her hair.

We had a den meeting the day the Wonderful Wiener Man came to town in his Frankmobile. When we expressed a unanimous desire to go down to Stop & Shop to meet him, my mother said it was fine with her, especially since she had some shopping to do anyway.

Before we left I ran upstairs and got my autograph book. My collection of signatures was getting to be impressive. Most of them came from obscure baseball players to whom I'd written fan letters, but a handful were from TV personalities who had recently visited Stop & Shop to promote their products. In the few months since the mini-mall's grand opening, I had met the Pillsbury Doughboy, Mr. Clean, Cap'n Crunch, and Chef Boy-R-Dee. I found it exciting to meet these characters in real life, just a few blocks from home. They were friendly, too. Baseball players at the stadium sometimes looked hurt or angry when you asked them to sign your scorecard, but the TV personalities were always delighted to chat, give autographs, and hand out free samples. I especially liked Mr. Clean, who had let me squeeze his biceps and rub his shiny head.

I expected good things from the Wiener Man. He was driving his Frankmobile to supermarkets all across America "to spread the wonderful word about Wonderful Wieners," a new brand of hot dog. In the past few days there had been a blitz of radio commercials publicizing his visit to our town. The commercials promised free food and lots of fun surprises.

It was a warm October day in 1969. We marched in double file to the mini-mall, our feet crunching down on the red and yellow leaves carpeting the sidewalk. My mother led the way. Her partner was Harold "the Dork" Daggett, the newest member of our den. Harold had only been with us a few weeks. He had just switched to public school from St. Agnes, and Mrs. Kerner had used that as an excuse to kick him out of the Catholic school den, where no one liked him anyway, and dump him on us. When we heard about the transfer we presented my mother with a petition saying Harold was a jerk and we didn't want him. My mother ripped the petition into confetti; Harold joined us the following week. We got our revenge by ignoring him when she was around and ganging up on him when she wasn't. She got her revenge, at least on me, by becoming good friends with him. She claimed that he was the smartest boy she'd ever met.

My partner was the den freak, Allen Falco. Allen had hair down to his shoulders and refused to wear the regulation cub scout uniform—he wore the shirt but substituted bell-bottom dungarees for the crisp blue trousers and tied the neckerchief around his head in an attempt to look like Jimi Hendrix. We were the last pair in line. I kept my eye on my mother as we walked. She kept smiling and touching Harold's shoulder. I heard her say, "That's fascinating, Harold."

Then Allen dropped a bombshell: a few nights ago, he said, when his Dad was out, he had seen his brother's girlfriend with her shirt off. Allen's brother was a hippie. He looked like Jesus and wore an army coat with a peace sign on the back. His girlfriend looked just like he did, minus the beard. Allen said that he got out of bed for a drink of water and she was just sitting there on the couch, watching TV with her tits hanging out. Allen was a good friend of mine, but I often had the feeling that our lives took place on different planets.

"So what happened?" I whispered.

"Nothing," he said. "I got a drink of water."

I walked straight into Billy Turcott, who bumped into Gary Zaleski in a chain reaction. My mother called a halt to our march.

"Harold has something he wants to share with us," she announced.

Harold stood beside her looking worried, his pudgy body stiff at attention. He wore thick glasses, and the left side of his shirt was decorated with merit badges and little gold stars. He had a squeaky voice.

"Even though we often think of hot dogs as an American food, they were actually invented way back in the Middle Ages in Frankfurt, West Germany. That's why we sometimes call them frankfurters. Another popular American food, the hamburger, is named for the German city of Hamburg."

Billy Turcott raised his hand. "Is there a German city called Dork?"

My mother frowned and Harold turned red. He looked like he wanted to cry but wasn't going to give us the pleasure of watching.

• • •

The Frankmobile was parked in the far corner of the lot, where Stop & Shop met Ye Olde Liquor Store. My heart sank when I saw it. I had taken the name seriously and expected to see a huge hot dog on wheels. But it was just a pink Winnebago.

My mother veered off from the group. "I'm going shopping," she said. "I'll meet you in front of the store in fifteen minutes."

We crossed the parking lot and got our first glimpse of the Wiener Man. He looked like a human hot dog, and kids were standing in line to shake his hand. Next to him, a woman from Stop & Shop stood behind a hot dog stand and passed out free Wonderful Wieners. The Wiener Man was taller than the yellow umbrella on the hot dog stand. We started walking faster.

The line formed between two rows of orange safety cones. There were about twenty kids ahead of us, most of them with their mothers. Not far from the Frankmobile, in front of Brite Boy Launderette, a bunch of tough-looking teenagers were slouched against a black GTO, smoking cigarettes and scowling at the Wiener Man like they knew him from somewhere and hated his guts.

While we waited, I tried to think up some good questions to ask him. I knew from experience that if you wanted to have a conversation with a celebrity, you had to get the ball rolling yourself. I made a mental list of the possibilities:

How did you get your job? Who do you like better—Joe Frazier or Muhammad Ali? Do you own a motorcycle? What's your favorite TV show? Were you ever in the service, and if so, what was your rank? Have you traveled to foreign countries? Do you know Chef Boy-R-Dee?

We were stuck in the middle of the line when Ricky Stoner, a kindergartner from our neighborhood, walked past us holding a Wonderful Wiener with both hands. He seemed to be concentrating deeply, like it was difficult to walk and carry a hot dog at the same time. Ricky got picked on a lot because something was wrong with his head—people said it was still soft, like a baby's—and his mother made him wear a Little League batting helmet all the time for protection. We called him Kazoo, after the Martian on *The Flintstones*, who also wore a funny helmet.

"Hey Kazoo," Billy Turcott called out. "Wait up."

Kazoo stopped. He tilted his head sideways like a dog to look at Billy.

"Whatcha got there?" Billy asked.

"Hot dog," said Kazoo. "They're free."

Billy stepped out of line and put his hand on Kazoo's shoulder, like the two of them were friends. "Can I have a bite?"

Kazoo glanced hopefully up at Billy and shook his head. Billy lifted his hand and slapped it down three times on the dome of Kazoo's blue helmet. Kazoo just stood there with his eyes squeezed shut and took it.

"Kazoo," Billy said thoughtfully, "do you want to be a cub scout next year?"

Kazoo nodded. He held the hot dog tightly to his chest. There was a little smear of mustard on his sweatshirt.

"Then you better give me a bite. It's your initiation."

"That's right," said Freddy DiLeo. "We all get a bite." Freddy was Billy's best friend.

Kazoo looked down at his Wonderful Wiener and up at seven cub scouts. The hot dog was only four bites big.

"He's lying!" Harold cried out. "There's no such thing as initiation."

"Shut up, Dork," Billy snapped. He glared at Kazoo. "Hand it over. Or else."

"Leave him alone, Billy," I said. "There's enough for everyone." I hadn't planned on saying anything, but after Harold spoke up, things looked different to me.

Kazoo sensed his chance and trotted away. Billy didn't chase after him. He got back in line and looked at me like I'd hurt his feelings. "What's the matter with you? I wasn't gonna take the little twerp's wiener."

"Oh yes you were," Harold said. His voice

was shaking. "You should pick on someone your own size."

"Oh yeah?" Billy poked Harold in the chest. "You're about my size, Dork." He hauled off and socked Harold in the arm, right above the elbow. Just from the sound you could tell it hurt. Harold didn't even say ouch; he just reached up and started rubbing. This time I kept my mouth shut.

Up close you could see that the Wiener Man was not as tall as he first appeared. His face was painted pink and stuck out of a hole in the middle of the hot dog suit. He wore a wiener-colored leotard and wiener-colored gloves. Only his dirty white sneakers kept him from being uniformly pink.

We were next in line. In front of us the Wiener Man posed for a picture with a little blonde girl in a red and white checkered dress. The two of them stood perfectly still with smiles frozen on their faces.

"Say cheese," said the girl's mother.

Just as she snapped the picture, one of the tough guys by the GTO flicked his cigarette at the Wiener Man. It arced through the air, sailed past the little girl's face, and landed on the blacktop at the Wiener Man's feet.

The tough guys laughed. There were four of them. The one who flicked the cigarette had long hair and a dirty peach-fuzz mustache. His faded dungaree jacket was covered with graffiti.

The Wiener Man gave the little girl back to her mother, then turned to the tough guys. He pointed to the cigarette. It was still lit; smoke curled up from it in a lazy **S**-shaped pattern.

"Does this belong to one of you gentlemen?" he asked.

"Maybe," said the guy who flicked it. "Maybe not." His friends laughed. They all had long hair parted in the middle, but the similarity ended there. One was chubby and red-faced. One reminded me of a rat. The third looked confused.

The Wiener Man's voice was calm. "Come over here and pick it up."

The tough guys looked at each other in disbelief. "Did you hear that?" the leader said. "Mr. Tube Steak wants me to pick up that butt."

The Rat touched his fly. "Yeah, I got a tube steak for him."

The woman from Stop & Shop stepped out from behind the cart and grabbed the Wiener Man's hand. "I'll go get the manager," she said.

"Forget the manager," he told her. "I can handle these guys myself."

I glanced at Allen. His eyes were wide with wonder. There was going to be a fight. This was more than we could have hoped for in our wildest dreams.

The Wiener Man put his hands where his hips must have been. His arms looked stumpy because they only stuck out from the elbows down. "Are you gonna come over here, or am I gonna go over there?"

"I think you're gonna have to come over here," said the tough guy.

"Okay." The Wiener Man walked slowly toward the GTO. The costume bunched up around his ankles, so he could only take tiny shuffling steps. The guy who flicked the cigarette put up his dukes and stepped forward. His friends stayed back by the car.

There was a momentary standoff. The Wiener Man towered over his opponent, but he didn't seem eager to take the first punch.

"Come on, weenie man," the tough guy sneered. "Put your money where your mouth is."

It wasn't much of a fight. The Wiener Man faked high with his left and came in low with his right, landing a solid gut shot that folded the tough guy right in half. When the punk was doubled over and gasping for air, the Wiener Man grabbed a hunk of his hair and led him over to the cigarette butt. When the tough guy picked it up, everyone cheered.

The Wiener Man called all seven of us up at once. After we introduced ourselves, he made a speech.

"Scouting's a fine thing," he said. "It'll give you direction in life, teach you the right values, keep you off the street. Whatever you do, don't grow up to be wiseguys. Wiseguys don't know it, but they're going nowhere fast."

He gave us a long serious look, then turned to the woman behind the hot dog stand. "Lois, why don't you give these fine young men a Wonderful Wiener on me. Boys, I'll be frank with you"—he winked for those of us who caught the joke—"in the world of wieners, they're the winners."

"I'd be glad to," said Lois. She took a bun out of the plastic bag and spread it apart on her palm with metal tongs.

The Wiener Man smiled when I asked for his autograph. "What's your name, son?" He scrawled his signature with confidence and flair, then snapped the book shut with my pen marking the page. "There you go." He handed it back to me.

He seemed friendly, so I decided to try one of my questions. "Sir," I said, "have you ever met Chef Boy-R-Dee?"

He didn't seem to hear me. He was gazing over my head at the doors of the Stop & Shop. I turned and saw my mother standing in front of the store, hugging a grocery bag with both arms, looking around for her scouts.

"Pardon me." The Wiener Man squeezed right between me and Allen. His suit was spongy to the touch. He shuffled through the parking lot as best he could, on a beeline for my mother. He had to move fast to dodge a long train of shopping carts. The kid pushing them wasn't paying attention.

"Ann," he called out. "Is that you?"

Ann was my mother's name.

My mother's face scrunched up above the groceries jutting out of the bag. Then she smiled. She had a really pretty smile. "Mike?" She didn't sound convinced.

The Wiener Man stuck out his little arms as he approached her. He hugged my mother right there in the parking lot. A can of tomato sauce spilled out of the bag and rolled toward Grand Avenue. I wanted to chase it, but my legs wouldn't move. My mother reached around with one hand and clutched a fistful of the wiener suit. I felt like everyone at the mini-mall was staring straight at me, demanding an explanation.

I removed the groceries one by one from the bag and handed them to my mother. She ranged gracefully around the kitchen, opening and closing cabinets, rearranging things according to her private system.

In the parking lot she had introduced the Wiener Man as Mr. Something-or-other, a friend of hers from high school. She held his wrist and blushed so deeply that her face was almost the same color as his.

He pointed to me. "This one must be yours, Ann. I recognize that mouth."

My mother laid her hand on my head. "This is Buddy. He's mine."

The Wiener Man sighed. "It's a small world, isn't it?"

My mother put her hand over her mouth and giggled. "I'm sorry, Mike. You just look so silly."

He nodded, his face moving independently inside the costume, and said he had to get back to work.

My mother opened the freezer door and stared for a long time at the jumble of ice cube trays and frozen meat. White vapors swirled around her head. If my father had been home, he would have yelled at her for wasting electricity.

"He was nice."

My words startled her. She shut the door without taking anything from the freezer. "I've always thought so," she said. She went to the table and plunged her arm into the empty bag. "Did you see a can of tomato sauce in here?"

"No."

"Darn," she said. "I'll have to make the pork chops. Your father won't be too thrilled about that."

While my mother cooked, I sat on the couch and read *Strange But True Football Stories*, a book I'd just checked out of the library. The first one was about Jim Marshall, a defensive end on the Minnesota Vikings, who picked up a fumble and ran the wrong way for a touchdown, actually scoring a safety for the other team. I couldn't make up my mind whether his mistake was funny or sad. He got spun around after picking up the loose ball and lost his bearings; the roar of the crowd drowned out his teammates' desperate cries. Marshall was totally happy as he ran: it was every lineman's dream, nothing but green grass between him and the end zone. He did a joyful touchdown dance and didn't begin to understand the enormity of his mistake until players from the other team swarmed all over him shouting congratulations. His own teammates clutched their helmets; the stadium echoed with laughter. Even the referee was smiling.

The phone rang in the kitchen. A few minutes later my mother came into the living room and asked if I was hungry. I told her I wasn't; I'd eaten a Wonderful Wiener before we left the mini-mall.

"Good," she said. "Mr. Amalfi wants us to drop by before he goes. I'll just stick the pork chops in the oven. We can pick up your father at the store and all eat together for once."

The mini-mall was almost deserted when we returned that evening. A few cars were clustered near the entrance of Stop & Shop. Beyond them, the Frankmobile stood alone in the corner of the lot. My mother squinted, as though it hurt her eyes to look at it.

"What a hideous color," she said. "It looks

like chewed-up bubble gum."

She glanced around to make sure no one was watching, then knocked on the side door. It swung open and the Wiener Man helped us climb inside. Only he wasn't the Wiener Man anymore. He was this normal-looking guy, just a little taller than my mother, wearing tan corduroy pants and a blue sweater. He had removed the gloves and scrubbed the makeup off his face. He was still wearing the beat-up sneakers.

The Frankmobile looked pretty big from the outside, but inside it was close and cluttered, like someone had taken an entire house and squashed it into one room. The three of us stood huddled between the door and the sink that jutted out from the opposite wall. The carpeted floor sagged beneath our weight.

The Wiener Man smiled at my mother. He had dark curly hair and a boyish face. "Ann," he said. "You look terrific. You haven't changed a bit."

"It's a nice place you got here," she said. She turned to get a better look and her purse swung into the side of my head.

"This is the kitchen," he said. "I don't use it much." There were cabinets above the sink and a tiny refrigerator next to the door. A small wooden table folded down from one wall. An unplugged toaster sat on top of it, along with a stack of magazines and a houseplant in a red clay pot.

"Let me give you the grand tour," said the Wiener Man.

The trailer swayed gently, like a boat, as we followed him through the bead curtain into his bedroom. We stood single file between the wall and the bed. There wasn't much to look at, except for a portable TV—it had aluminum foil flags attached to the rabbit ears—plopped in the middle of the sunken mattress. My mother asked the Wiener Man about his parents.

"Pop passed away two years ago," he said. "Cancer."

"I wish I'd known," she said. "I could've at least sent a card."

"It was bad," he said. "We weren't even on speaking terms when he died. He never forgave me for not taking over the business."

"How's your mother?"

"She's a pain in the ass, as usual. All she does is complain. Like I don't have enough problems of my own."

He opened the bathroom door. My mother peeked inside and laughed. I couldn't see what she was looking at.

I sat next to my mother on a padded bench behind the kitchen table and played a game called Hi-Q while she talked to the Wiener Man. It was a neat game, something like Chinese checkers, but harder. The Wiener Man told me that he used to spend hours playing it on nights when he couldn't sleep. After a while it got too easy for him, so he took up crossword puzzles.

I listened to their conversation between jumps. Mostly it was about people I'd never heard of. Harvey owned an appliance store. Dolly finally got divorced from Phil. Someone named "Neemo" got transferred to Chicago. Angie had three beautiful daughters and a no-good husband. They both laughed when she told him that Louise had married a dentist, this little dumpy guy.

I didn't get the joke, but I laughed anyway. I was really enjoying myself. I liked the coziness and dim light inside the Frankmobile, the feeling of being hidden from the world but not alone. It reminded me of a trip I'd taken with my parents the summer after kindergarten. We rented a pop-up camper—the kind that emerges magically from a box when you turn the crank—and took it to Cooperstown, New York. It rained the whole time we were there, but we didn't mind. We spent our days browsing through the Baseball Hall of Fame, touching old uniforms, buying souvenirs, talking to Babe Ruth on a special telephone. We couldn't barbecue because of the weather, so we ate all our meals at this diner that had a revolving glass case filled with the biggest cakes and pies I'd ever seen. When we got back to the camper my father would fall right to sleep, but my mother and I stayed up late playing Go Fish by flashlight, whispering our questions and answers over my father's slow breathing and the steady patter of rain on the roof.

Staring at the Hi-Q board and listening to their voices, I let myself imagine we were a family. It seemed like a fun way to live, a permanent vacation, the three of us inside the Frankmobile, playing games and eating out all the time. I saw us zooming down the highway, a pink blur passing through a landscape of cactus and snow-capped mountains on our way to the next supermarket. But I saw something else, too: my real father wandering through our house, checking in the closets and under the bed, wondering where we'd gone without him.

My mother touched my hand. "Buddy, Mr. Amalfi wants to know if we're happy."

I shrugged. "Sure. I guess so."

She laughed and messed my hair, like I'd just done something cute. She pretended to count on her fingers. "I can't believe it, Mike. I've been married for nine years now."

"That's a long time," said the Wiener Man.

"I wish you could meet Jim," she said. "I think you'd like him."

The Wiener Man nodded. "Jim's a lucky man."

"What about you?" she asked. "Are you happy?"

He uncrossed his legs and sat up straight on top of his little woodgrain refrigerator. "Happy?" he repeated, as if he hadn't understood the question. "I don't know about that. This is a decent job. I like seeing the country and meeting the kids. But it gets kind of lonely sometimes."

"Why don't you get married?" my mother said. "You're still young."

"I don't feel so young," said the Wiener Man.

There was a long lull in the conversation. They just looked at each other. My mother took the gray purse from her lap and set it on the table. She unclasped it and took out her wallet. I thought she was going to give some money to the Wiener Man, but she looked at me instead.

"Buddy, could you do me a favor? Run into Stop & Shop and pick up a can of tomato sauce, okay? Contadina. The smaller can, not the big huge one. That's in aisle six." She pressed a crumpled dollar into my hand. "You can get a candy bar with the change."

I glanced at the Hi-Q board. There was no way I could win. "Right now?" I asked.

She nodded. "Wait for me outside. I'll only be a few more minutes."

I stepped out from behind the table. The Wiener Man stared glumly at his feet. I wanted to cheer him up.

"Tell her about that kid you pounded today," I suggested.

. . .

The night had grown cooler. High up, the sky remained a deep daytime blue, but near the ground it was dark. All the lights were on in the parking lot. I went over to the front window of Stop & Shop and stood on tiptoe to peer inside the dazzling store. I couldn't see any customers, just two checkout girls in green smocks talking across three empty counters.

I shoved the dollar into my pocket and hopped a ride on a nearby shopping cart. I glided toward Grand Avenue, gathering speed on the downward slope. I found the can of tomato sauce right where I thought it would be, lying against a concrete parking barrier. It wasn't even dented.

I walked past the Frankmobile and sat down on the curb in front of the launderette. I amused myself by tossing the can into the air with one hand and catching it with the other, enjoying the swift pull of gravity as it smacked into my palm. Across Grand Avenue, a chalky fingernail moon hung at a strange tilt over the jagged line of house-tops.

"Hi."

The voice came from Harold Daggett. Like me, he was still wearing his uniform. He was also carrying a gym bag. "I saw you sitting here," he explained. He sat down beside me and set the gym bag between his feet. "Thanks for sticking up for me today. I didn't think you liked me."

"You were right," I said. "Billy was acting like a jerk."

Harold looked at the Frankmobile. "Is he nice?"

"Yeah, pretty nice. My mom's in there."

"I want to go with him," Harold said.

"You mean like running away?"

Harold nodded. "I hate it here. You think he'll take me with him?"

"I'm not sure," I told him. "Probably."

We didn't talk for a while. The parking lot was flat and empty, almost like a lake, except for a few stray shopping carts that here and there gleamed silver in the artificial light.

"By the way," I said, "it was interesting what you told us today. That stuff about hot dogs and hamburgers."

"Oh that." He shrugged. "It was in the encyclopedia."

Seconds later, the door of the Frankmobile swung open. My mother stepped down onto the pavement.

"Buddy?" she called out.

I walked into the light, leaving Harold behind me, alone and invisible in the shadows.

"We're late," my mother said. "We have to walk fast."

My father was the assistant manager at a store called Lamp City. It was located just a few blocks from the mini-mall, on an otherwise deserted part of Grand Avenue. After dark you could see it from far away, a small solitary building surrounded by a smoky yellow halo.

There must have been a thousand lamps in there. They hung from the ceiling, stood on the floor, rested on shelves and tables. My father hated it. The glare hurt his eyes and gave him headaches. He tried wearing sunglasses for a while, but his boss got mad. When he got home at night, he sat in his chair in the living room and ate dinner in the dark. Some nights his eyes were so sore he couldn't bear to watch TV or read the paper.

He waited with his hands and face pressed against the front window. His expression changed when he saw us. He smiled and raised one finger, then disappeared in toward the rear of the store. When he hit the master switch, that whole galaxy of lamps went black. My mother turned to me in the sudden darkness and asked if I had done my homework.

# Thirteen

"It's foolproof," Kevin explained. "If someone comes in and buys fifteen dollars worth of gas, I just ring up five and keep ten for myself."

"What about the pump?" I asked. "Doesn't that keep track?"

"Not really. It just goes back to zero every time you flip the switch."

Gas was expensive that summer, in 1974, and for a few weeks we were rich. Kevin bought me albums, food, and sporting goods with the money he stole from Paul's Amoco. He paid his brother's friend Burnsy to drive us to Yankee Stadium and Bowcraft Amusement Park. Every time I returned from one of these excursions I told my mother the same half-lie. I said that Paul had paid for everything.

Paul was Kevin's new stepfather. He had met Mrs. Ross on the supermarket checkout line in February and married her in March. When he moved in, he bought Kevin a fantastic ten-speed bike and tried to be his friend. But Kevin didn't want to be friends. He claimed that Paul was a sex maniac.

"Listen to this," Kevin said, just a few weeks after the wedding. He slipped a cassette into his tape player and cranked up the volume. All I could hear was loud static with vague murmurs in the background.

"What is it?"

"They're humping." he said. "Can't you tell?"

He rewound the tape. The murmurs turned into soft moans and deep sighs. I had a hard time connecting these sounds with Kevin's mother, a thin quiet woman who smoked extra-long cigarettes and told him to be careful every time he left the house.

"I swear," he said. "It's all they ever do."

Kevin's real father had died a long time ago. He had been an amateur boxer. Kevin had once come to a Halloween party dressed in gym shorts and boxing gloves, with his father's jockstrap and huge protective cup fitted over his head like a mask. Whenever someone asked him what he was, he lifted the cup away from his face with his fat leather thumbs and said, "I'm a dick, what are you?"

A sticky heat wave rolled in early that summer, right after school let out. We got in the habit of going to Kevin's house in the afternoon to watch re-

• • •

I was with Kevin at the St. Agnes carnival in Cranwood the night he first laid eyes on Angela Farrone. We were standing by the food booths,
spearing french fries from a paper cone.

"Look at that," he said. "By the Porta-John."

She was a gum-snapping bleached blond
about our age, a knockout in a white tube top and
jeans so tight that Kevin said she probably had to
pack herself in with a shoehorn. In one hand she
held a green helium balloon on a string, in the
other a goldfish in a little plastic bag filled with
water. The door of the Porta-John popped open
and a scrawny redhead stepped out, glancing
sheepishly around. She took the balloon from her
friend and the two of them entered the moving
crowd, like cars merging with highway traffic.

We followed them past the bake sale, the
wheels of fortune, and the creaky rent-a-rides,
then out of the carnival and down a sidestreet lit-
tered with ripped tickets and greasy paper plates.
They stopped beneath a streetlight, huddling together with their backs turned in our direction.
The green balloon jerked up and down above
their heads. We caught up with them just as they
stepped apart, hands empty at their sides. For one
miraculous moment the balloon and the fish were
suspended in midair, connected by the string.
Then they started to rise.

We stood with our heads back, watching the

balloon gain altitude as it drifted upward and east-
ward over the treetops, toward New York City.
The goldfish glinted orange in the light, then disappeared, like a match flaring out.

"Hey," Kevin said. "Why'd you do that?"

The blond shrugged. "The last time I brought
a fish home, my Dad flushed it down the toilet."

Kevin called Angela every night for a week, but
she kept hanging up on him. Then he had an idea.
He bought a dozen roses and hired me—I was
good in school—to write her a letter.

> Dear Angela,
>     My name is Kevin Ross and I have a crush
> on you. We met on Friday night outside the
> Carnival. I've been thinking about your fish.
> Maybe it got lucky and fell in a lake! Will you
> please come to the movies with me sometime
> soon? We can see anything you want.
>     Your (hopefully) friend,
>     Kevin Ross
>     P.S.—In case you're wondering, I've em-
> ployed a friend to give us a ride.

Kevin paid me ten dollars for the letter and another ten for delivery, five of which went to
Burnsy, who drove me to Angela's house in the
ritzy section of Cranwood. It was early evening,
and a sprinkler spun jets of water across the plush

front lawn. The shrubs near the house had been trimmed to look like gum drops and spinning tops. I set the roses on the welcome mat, then turned and ran back to Burnsy's Duster.

Kevin and Angela went to the drive-in on their first date. They really hit it off. Burnsy said there was so much heavy breathing in the back seat that he had to get out of the car and watch the second half of *Billy Jack* sitting on the gravel, holding the speaker to his ear. He told me this as we drove to Angela's to deliver another bouquet of roses, along with a poem I'd written at White Diamond:

> Last night at the drive-in
> The people in cars
> Were watching the movie
> But we were the stars!

It was Wednesday afternoon and I should have been doing my paper route. I was a carrier for the *Community News*, a freebie shopper paper. Once a week I had to fold 300 papers, secure them with rubber bands, then deliver one to every house in a six-block area. The entire process took about seven hours, and I made ten bucks.

I had been wobbling down Oak Street around noon on my old stingray bike when Burnsy's car pulled up and began crawling down the street beside me. Kevin rolled down the passenger window. I could tell from his greasy T-shirt that he was on lunch hour from the station.

"Hey Buddy," he said. "You ever write a poem?"

"Nope."

"Think you could handle it?"

I whizzed a paper at someone's front porch, just a little too hard. It slammed into the screen door: dogs started barking up and down the street.

"Sure," I said. "No sweat. Just let me finish up."

He leaned out the window and waved some money in my face.

"Come on," he told me. "I'll make it worth your while."

At the corner, Burnsy opened his trunk and threw my bike and canvas bag inside. By the time we got back from Angela's, I didn't feel like finishing my route. I went home, stuffed the last fifty papers into my bag, and rode out to the woods behind Indian Park. I dumped the papers into the brook, then sat down under a tree to leaf through a copy of *Playboy* someone had thoughtfully left behind.

"Sue really likes you," Angela whispered. "Do you like her?"

"I don't know," I said. "We just met."

Sue was the redhead. Her parents were away for the weekend, and her older sister had agreed to let us have the house to ourselves on Friday night. It was my job to keep her occupied so Kevin could be alone with Angela.

Sue and I sat rigidly on the love seat while Kevin and Angela huddled together on the couch, holding hands and playing games with their fingers. Angela smoked like an old movie star, closing one eye and shooting a slender jet of smoke at the plastic-covered lampshade. She was wearing a turquoise tube top, and I felt a pang of sadness. Sue was okay. She had thick red hair and a cute face. But Angela! I must have been staring, because she smiled at me and stuck out her tongue.

"Hey," Kevin said. "Let's play spin the bottle."

It was a surprising suggestion. None of us had ever played before, and Kevin had to explain the rules. I got Sue on the first spin of the game. Embarrassed, I craned my neck and planted a quick dry peck on the corner of her mouth. Kevin booed.

"What kind of a kiss was that?"

Sue spun next and got Kevin. Their mouths were so wide open it looked more like artificial respiration than making out. When they finally unstuck their faces, Kevin collapsed to the floor. Sue wiped her mouth and grinned.

Angela's kiss had a sweet, complicated taste. I felt her tongue working its way between my teeth and then something else, something soft and loose, and the next thing I knew her gum had slipped into my mouth, a secret gift. We kept going until Kevin wrenched us apart.

Angela fanned her face with one hand. "Whew," she said. "Who turned up the heat?"

The game ended on the next spin. Kevin and Angela started on their knees, then tipped over and stretched out on the floor. Five minutes passed, and they still hadn't surfaced for air.

Sue smiled apologetically. "Well," she said. "Looks like you're stuck with me."

We kissed for a while, then decided to go for a walk. We ended up sitting on the swings at a playground down the street. It was a beautiful night, the whole world at room temperature.

"I'm sorry Kevin dragged you here," she said.

"He didn't drag me. I wanted to come."

"Right." She pushed off and started swinging lazily back and forth. "Angela always tries to fix me up with her boyfriends' friends."

"Does she have a lot of boyfriends?"

"Pretty many. The last one was nineteen. Her father threw a shit fit when he found out."

"Nineteen," I said. "That's incredible."

"I know," said Sue. "But I think she really likes Kevin. He sends her flowers and writes her these sweet little poems. I wish someone would do that for me."

I didn't say anything. I just sat there chewing Angela's bland gum, thinking about her and Kevin.

"I'm scared of going to high school," she said. "Aren't you?"

"I'm not going yet."

She seemed surprised. "How old are you?"

"I'll be thirteen next week."

"Huh," she said. "I thought you were older."

She hopped off the swing and cartwheeled into a handstand. Her shirt came untucked, exposing a band of creamy skin.

"Come on," she called out. "Let's go home."

Sue walked effortlessly on her hands for an entire block, her palms slapping out a rubbery rhythm on the sidewalk. At the corner she arched forward like a Slinky and snapped into an upright position. We went back to her house and played Ping-Pong until Burnsy showed up to drive us home. Kevin was quiet in the back seat. Midway through the ride, he tapped me on the shoulder and handed me a ten-dollar bill.

We had planned to go to Bowcraft Amusement Park on Monday night—play a round of miniature golf, take some cuts at the batting cage, feed a few quarters to the pinball machine. But when Burnsy's car swung into the Little League parking lot, I could tell something was wrong.

"Where's Kevin?" I asked.

"Back here."

I leaned over the headrest and saw him lying on the floor between the seats, his head poking out from underneath a green army blanket.

"I'm dead," he told me. "The accountant came today and Paul found out about the money.

I think he knows it was me."

"Did he say anything?"

"No, but you should have seen the way he was staring."

I felt myself getting angry. It was fun being rich, doing something different every night, writing stuff for money. I wasn't ready for it to end. In less than a month I'd managed to save almost fifty bucks, but that wasn't nearly enough for the ten-speed bike I was hoping to buy.

"I thought you said it was foolproof," I snapped.

"Christ, Buddy. I didn't know he had a fucking *accountant*."

"So what are you going to do?"

"I can't go home," he said. "Paul's gonna kill me."

He spent the night in Burnsy's car. The next morning Burnsy drove him to Seaside, where Kevin figured he could stay with his brother until Paul had a chance to cool off. But when they finally located the house where Jack was supposed to be staying, they found out that he had split for Florida with this chick he'd picked up on the beach.

"So where's Kevin now?" I asked Burnsy later that night.

"Come on," Burnsy said. "I'll show you."

He parked his car on Center Street and led me into Indian Park. At the edge of the bike path, he stuck two fingers in his mouth and whistled. The signal was returned from inside the woods.

"Go in about a hundred yards and take the left fork," he told me.

"Aren't you coming?" I asked.

Burnsy shook his head. "I'm going back to Seaside. They said I could have Jack's room." He kicked some gravel and told me to take it easy.

Kevin was waiting for me on the main path, his blond hair and white T-shirt radiating a ghostly light, seeming to float disembodied on the darkness.

"Boy," he said. "Am I glad to see you."

He had a pup tent set up in a small clearing, its fluorescent orange fabric camouflaged by a web of tree branches and uprooted weeds. We sat together on a half-rotten log and made plans for Kevin's new life as a fugitive. I promised to keep him well-stocked with food, to deliver messages to Angela, and not to reveal his hiding place even if Paul tried to torture me for the information, which Kevin claimed was a definite possibility. Everything was okay as long as we kept talking. But as soon as our conversation died out, the woods turned spooky. A million insects hummed together; small animals darted through the underbrush.

Kevin slapped his leg. "Damn! I wish I had some bug spray."

"I'll get you some tomorrow," I said, standing up from the log.

His fingers wrapped around my ankle. "Hey," he said, "why don't you go home and tell your parents that you're sleeping over at my house. Then you can get your sleeping bag and come back here. It'll be like that camping trip."

"Not tonight, Kev. I have to fold my papers."

His grip tightened. "Please, Buddy. Just this once?"

I shook my leg free. "I can't."

There was a long pause. The insects turned up the volume. I was glad I couldn't see Kevin's face.

"Thanks a lot, Buddy. After everything I've given you, you can't even do me this one little favor."

"Hey," I said, "no one told you to rip off your own family."

I went home and folded my papers on the living room floor. My parents sat behind me on the couch, laughing along with the canned laughter on television.

"Happy birthday!"

My mother woke me the next morning with a lipsticky kiss on the cheek. It was August 8, 1974, and I was officially thirteen years old. It was something I'd been waiting for for a long time.

"Don't make any plans for tonight," she said. "We have a surprise for you."

After she left for work, I wolfed down a bowl of cereal and hopped, still half asleep, onto my bike. I wanted to finish my paper route as quickly as possible so I could spend the afternoon with Kevin. I hoped he wasn't mad at me.

Around eleven o'clock a brown tow truck turned the corner and began tailgating me down Maple Street. I veered up a driveway to give it room, but the truck didn't accelerate to pass. Then I saw why: "PAUL'S AMOCO EMERGENCY SERVICE" was written in yellow letters on the side door. Paul himself was scowling at me from the driver's seat, jabbing his finger like a cop pulling over a speeding car. I stepped on the brakes and so did he. The truck's passenger door swung open on a creaky hinge.

"Get in," he commanded.

"What about my bike?"

"Just leave it."

I dropped my bike on someone's lawn and climbed into the cab, which smelled pleasantly of gasoline. Paul sat beside me, pinching the bridge of his nose between his thumb and forefinger. The skin on his knuckles was cracked, the crevices caked with grease. He took his hand away from his face and looked at me.

"Where's Kevin?"

"Isn't he home?" I tried to sound casual, but I could feel my blood abruptly reverse itself, rushing into my face as though I were doing a headstand.

Paul gave me a disgusted look and shifted into gear. I wondered vaguely if I was being kidnapped.

"It's not the money that bugs me," he said. "It's really not. But if he needed it, why didn't he just ask?"

I didn't answer. How could I explain that Kevin didn't *need* the money, that we were just having fun?

"Tell me the truth," Paul said. "Is he doing drugs?"

I shook my head. It gradually became clear to me that I wasn't being kidnapped. We were just orbiting the streets of Darwin, cruising up one and down another. I began to relax and enjoy the ride, my first ever in a tow truck. The heavy chains swayed and clanked behind us; our bodies vibrated along with the powerful engine. The parked cars we passed looked small and vulnerable. If Paul and I had felt like it, we could have just hoisted one up and dragged it away.

"How come he hates me?" Paul asked.

"I don't know," I said.

He took a couple of quick turns, and pretty soon we were back on Maple. I was almost disappointed that nothing more exciting had happened, that Paul hadn't tried to make me talk. I had one leg out the door when he grabbed my arm.

"You tell Kevin to come home. He's not going to get punished. We just want him back. You tell him his mother's worried sick."

"Okay," I said.

I got out, walked over to my bike, and slung the heavy canvas bag over my shoulder. The tow truck didn't move. Paul was slumped forward in the driver's seat, his forehead resting on the wheel.

That afternoon I told Kevin about my encounter with Paul. He was only half finished with the sandwich I'd brought him, but he got mad and whipped it at a tree.

"He's a liar! The second I walk through the door he's gonna kill me."

"I bet he won't."

"You don't know him."

We sat sullenly on the log. The woods weren't the least bit scary during the day. Birds were chirping; the air was cool and fresh. You could see through the trees to the houses on Center Street.

"Can you camp out tonight?" Kevin asked.

"Tonight's my birthday," I said. "I promised my parents I'd spend it at home."

Kevin looked tired. His eyes were bloodshot, his hair matted down against his head. "But what about later? Think you can sneak out?"

"I'll try."

Before I left, Kevin asked me to do him a favor. He unzipped the flap of his tent—not very well camouflaged during the day—and pulled out a wrinkled envelope, which he handed to me along with a crisp twenty-dollar bill. Angela's name was scrawled across the envelope in big childish letters.

"I wrote it myself," he said.

People's houses have distinctive odors. Kevin's, for example, always reminded me of a doctor's office. Burnsy's smelled like cat food, even though he didn't have a cat. My grandmother's house gave off an odor of rancid orange peels. And the Farrones' house smelled like Angela. As soon as I stepped inside, I remembered that when I had kissed her, her mouth had tasted exactly like *this*.

I followed her father down the hallway into the kitchen. On the way I caught a glimpse of the living room. It resembled a display in a furniture store, not a cushion dented or an ashtray out of place. An oil portrait of Angela, done before she bleached her hair, was hanging above the couch. In her tartan plaid dress with the lace collar, this brown-haired Angela looked innocent and full of wonder.

Mr. Farrone tossed my bouquet carelessly on the kitchen table and headed for the refrigerator. It was the modern kind that dispensed ice water from a compartment on the freezer door. I had only seen them on commercials and game shows, never in someone's house.

"What can I get you?" he asked.

"Just water."

On my previous flower deliveries, I had managed to escape undetected. But that afternoon my timing was off. I was halfway up the front steps when a maroon Lincoln Continental pulled into the driveway. A dumpy man in a gray suit got out of the car and came to meet me.

"I'm Pat Farrone," he said, extending his hand. "You must be Kevin."

I started to say no, then caught myself and nodded. It seemed easier not to have to explain the situation.

"Here," I said, thrusting the roses into his arms. "These are for Angela."

Mr. Farrone cradled the roses like a baby. He had heavy jowls and a mustache that looked like a misplaced eyebrow. It seemed bizarre to me that such an odd-looking man could have a daughter as beautiful as Angela.

"Kevin," he said, "I think you and I need to have a talk."

Mr. Farrone sat at the head of the table, stroking his mustache. His voice was calm and professional, as though he were interviewing me for a job.

"How old are you, Kevin?"

"Thirteen," I said.

"Thirteen." He nodded solemnly. "You know, Kevin, when I was thirteen I wasn't chasing girls. All I wanted to do was play baseball."

He lifted the flowers to his nose, sniffed them, and frowned. When he set them back down, he inadvertently rotated the bouquet, so the envelope with Angela's name was now facing up.

"Roses are expensive, Kevin. Where do you get your money?"

"My Dad owns a gas station. He lets me work there."

"Tell me, Kevin. What do you want to do with your life?"

"I'm not sure. I think I'd like to be a park ranger. Either that or a truck driver."

"My daughter tells me you're quite the little poet."

"Thanks."

I was blushing with pride when he reached out and casually detached the envelope from the wrapping paper on the bouquet. He jammed his finger into the flap and began tearing it open, as though it were addressed to him. He stopped halfway through and glanced at me.

"That was a helluva hickey you gave her the other night."

"A hickey?" I said.

"Don't bullshit me, Kevin. I don't like bull-shitters."

I should have been alarmed, but I had this funny feeling that I wasn't really there, that all this was happening to Kevin, not to me. Mr. Farrone unfolded the sheet of loose-leaf paper and spread it flat on the table. He squinted at the words. A vertical fold appeared in his forehead.

"You little bastard," he whispered.

For a heavy man he was nimble. Before I understood what was happening, he was out of his chair. He grabbed a handful of my T-shirt and yanked me to my feet. We danced awkwardly across the linoleum floor until my back slammed into the humming refrigerator.

"I oughta knock your teeth out," he said softly. "She's just a little girl."

His face was so close to mine I could feel hot bursts of air coming from his nostrils. A muscle in his cheek began to twitch. I watched his hand form itself into a fist. "What kind of rubbers did you buy, smart guy? Why don't you take them out of your wallet and show me?"

This isn't happening to me, I told myself, but the formula had lost its magic. All at once I was terribly frightened, not just for me but for Kevin too.

"Come on, big man. Show me your rubbers."

"I don't have any," I told him. "I don't even know what they look like."

"I oughta knock your teeth out," he said again, drawing back his fist until it was level with his ear. His knuckles were coated with thick black hair. "What do you say to that, big man?"

I had spent the past several years learning not to cry, but I hadn't forgotten how. My bottom lip trembled. My eyes felt like they were growing inside my head. The first few sobs came from somewhere deep in my stomach. A jet of warm snot exploded from my nose.

"I'm a kid," I blubbered. "I'm just a kid."

Mr. Farrone lowered his fist and let go of my shirt. He stepped back and looked at the floor, as though he were ashamed for both of us.

"Jesus Christ," he said, then went and got me a Kleenex.

My father wheeled the bicycle into the living room. My mother stood behind him, smiling nervously.

"Happy birthday," they said.

This was definitely not the bike I wanted. It was a Schwinn three-speed, clunky and old-fashioned, with a chain guard, lots of chrome, and a two-tone seat straight out of *Happy Days*.

"Thanks," I said, forcing a smile.

"It'll be much easier to do your papers," my mother said hopefully.

My father slapped the seat. "She's a beauty. Why don't you take her for a spin."

"It's getting dark," I said. "Maybe tomorrow."

A wounded look flashed across my mother's face. My father gave me the raspberry.

"Hey," he said, "if you won't, I will."

My mother held open the front door as he lugged the bike outside. I got out of the recliner and followed them down the front steps to the edge of the driveway. My father straddled the crossbar.

"Here goes nothing," he said.

"Be careful," my mother called out.

He got off to a shaky start. The handlebars swiveled from side to side, and the bike followed an invisible slalom course down the sidewalk.

"He fell in love with that bike the moment he saw it," my mother said. "I hope you like it."

"I do," I said. "It's really nice."

My father turned around at the corner and headed back in the street, looking much steadier on his return. He was grinning and breathing hard when he dismounted.

"Give 'er a whirl," he told me. "She's got some pep."

As much as I hated to admit it, he was right. The fat tires hummed, and the bike, heavy as it was, floated luxuriously on the blacktop. I could go as fast as I wanted.

The sky darkened as I pedaled past houses, stores, and factories, shifting through my three new gears. If Kevin had been home, I would've gone straight to his house to show him my birthday present. He would've laughed and taken it for a test ride. Instead he was sitting on a log in the woods, listening to the spooky night.

Somehow I ended up in front of his house anyway. It was as if the bike had taken me there of its own accord. My legs felt hollow as I climbed the front steps. The doorbell button was glowing orange, like a lit cigarette.

• • •

I had been gone for a long time, but my father was still waiting for me on the front stoop when I got back.

"How'd you like it?" he asked.

"It's great. I didn't want to get off."

"Man," he said, "what I wouldn't have given for a bike like that when I was your age."

We each took a handlebar and wheeled my new bike up the driveway. My father had cleared a place for it inside the toolshed.

"I looked at the ten-speeds," he told me, "but they cost an arm and a leg. Besides, what do you need ten speeds for?"

"I don't know," I said.

Before we went inside, we stood for a few minutes in the backyard, gazing up at the stars. It was a clear, moonless night. The Big Dipper, one of the few constellations I knew, was blazing in the sky like an upside-down question mark.

I had just ratted on my best friend. At that very moment, Kevin was probably walking out of the woods between his mother and Paul, and I didn't know if he was going to hate me or thank me. My father put his hand on my shoulder.

"Thirteen," he said, as if that explained everything.

# Race Riot

The way I heard it, these two black guys crashed the teen dance in the Little League parking lot. One of them had a funny hat, a red sailor's cap pulled down over his eyes. The other was tall and skinny. At first they just hung out near the band, jiving and nodding their heads to the music.

In 1975 Darwin was still an all-white town, a place where blacks were not welcome after dark. It must have taken a certain amount of courage for the two guys just to thread their way through the crowd, knowing they were being watched and whispered about, maybe even pointed at. The focus of the dance shifted with their arrival, until the whole event came to revolve around the mystery of their presence. Did they like the music? Were they looking for trouble?

Nobody really minded until they started bugging Margie and Lorraine. Later Margie said it was no big deal, they just wanted to dance. But she

47

was wearing these incredible cutoffs, and Sammy Rizzo and some of the other football players didn't like the way the black guys were staring at her ass. There would have been trouble right then, but a cop stepped in when it was still a shouting match and sent the brothers home.

I'd left the dance early with Tina, so I didn't see any of this happen. I didn't even hear about it until Tuesday afternoon, when Sammy Rizzo slapped me on the back and asked if I was ready to rumble.

"Rumble?" I said. The word sounded old-fashioned and vaguely goofy to me, like "jitter-bug" or "Daddy-o," something the Fonz might say on *Happy Days*.

"Yeah," he said. "Tonight at eight. Better bring a weapon."

I didn't own any weapons except for a Swiss army knife that seemed completely unsuitable for a rumble, so I had to improvise from a selection of garden tools hanging in my parents' toolshed. My choice—a short, three-pronged fork used for weeding—was a big hit at the Little League.

"Jesus Christ," said Sammy. "That looks like something outta James Bond."

"Yeah," Mike Caravello observed. "You could probably rip someone's balls off with that."

We were sitting on picnic tables inside the pavilion, waiting for the baseball game to end. Caravello sat next to me, twisting his class ring around and around his finger. He made a fist and the ring's red jewel jutted up from his hand, a freak knuckle.

"Some nigger's gonna get Class of '74 tattooed on his face," he said, flashing a nasty silver grin. He was way too old to be wearing braces.

A jacked–up Impala squealed into the parking lot behind the first-base bleachers. Caravello pounded the tabletop.

"Fuckin' excellent! It's the twins!"

The twins got out of the car and looked around, using their hands for visors. They were both wearing overalls with no shirts underneath, and their muscles were all pumped up from lifting.

"Which one's Danny?" I asked.

"The one with the tire iron," Caravello said.

My chest tightened up. Until that moment, the fight had seemed like a game to me, a new way to kill a night. But the twins were serious brawlers. They hurt people for fun. Caravello called them over so he could introduce me.

"This is Joey T.'s cousin, Buddy," he said. "He's gonna be frosh QB next year."

The twins nodded. They had shoulder–length hair and identical blank faces, like a genetic tag team. I couldn't imagine playing football with people their size.

Danny scratched his head with the tip of the tire iron.

"Joey comin' tonight?"

"He can't," I explained. "He's eighteen now.

If he gets busted, they won't let him be a cop."

Danny's brother, Paul, asked to see my weeding implement. Its three prongs were bent and sharpened, forming a sort of metal claw.

"Wow," he said. "You could tear somebody's eyes out with this."

The twins made fourteen of us. Our ranks, I noticed, were pretty much split: half normal guys, half psychos. The normal guys—I considered myself one—were just trying to defend our hangout. The psychos were looking for a good time.

The Rat Man, Sean Fallon, was busy picking his teeth with the rusty tip of his switchblade. I couldn't even look at him without getting the creeps. He got his nickname from his habit of biting people in fights. A few months before, for no good reason, he had bitten off Ray Malone's nipple in the middle of what was supposed to be a friendly wrestling match. A cop had to drive the nipple to the hospital so the doctors could surgically reattach it to Ray's chest. I heard that he carried it into the emergency room in a small white envelope. Norman LaVerne sat next to the Rat Man, frowning and shaking his head. Years ago, when he'd lived in another town, people said that Norman had buried a cat from the neck down and run over its head with a lawn mower. Normally I crossed the street when I saw him coming. But tonight we were on the same side.

"TWO, FOUR, SIX, EIGHT, WHO DO
WE APPRECIATE?"

Baseball hats, purple and red, flew into the sky
and fluttered down. The players and spectators
slowly drifted out of the park. I could feel the tension gather. We stopped talking and fixed our eyes
on the paths that led through the woods to the
Washington Avenue section of Cranwood, where
the blacks lived.

At five to eight, two cop cars drove into the
park from separate entrances and converged on the
pavilion. Jim Bruno got out of the lead car. He
was the greatest running back our town had ever
produced; people still called him the Bulldozer. I
remembered going to games with my father and
watching him plow through the defense, play after
play, dragging tacklers for yards before going
down. He had a mustache now, and the begin-
nings of a donut gut.

"Fight won't happen," he announced.

Nobody moved.

"You want me to put it in sign language?"

He looked at the ground and spat neatly between his polished shoes.

The Camaro was brand-new, gleaming white,
with a plush red interior and a wicked eight-track
system. Caravello's parents had given it to him as a
graduation present even though he hadn't graduated. In September he would begin his fifth year of

high school. Technically, he was still a sophomore.

We cruised down North Avenue, Deep Purple blasting from our open windows. I liked Caravello when he let me ride in his car. The rest of the time I had my doubts about him. He didn't have any friends his own age, and I resented his success with the girls who hung out with us at the park. I especially hated the way he turned on you when a girl showed up. He had this trick of turning his class ring so the jewel faced out from his palm, and then clapping you on the head with it.

Caravello turned down the music as we passed the lumber yard.

"Fuckin' quarterback," he said. "Every cheerleader in the world will want to suck your cock."

"Not quite," I said.

He waved me off. "You don't know shit. Those football parties are wild."

I thought about the stories I'd heard.

"Is it true about Margie Waldman?"

Caravello grinned. I could see the rubber bands inside his mouth, white with spittle. "What'd you hear about Margie Waldman?"

"You know. That she did it with the whole starting team after the Thanksgiving game."

"Not the whole team," he said. "Just the defense."

We stopped at a red light in front of the perforating company. Two huge fans blew factory exhaust straight into the car. Outside, swing shifters in rumpled green clothes sat against the red brick building and ate their lunches. They chewed slowly and gazed at us without interest.

"Stupid assholes," Caravello said. When the light turned green, he laid a patch.

Just before we reached downtown Elizabeth, Caravello pulled a U-turn and headed home. Beyond the smokestacks and water towers, the last streaks of color were dissolving in the sky. Instead of continuing straight into town, we turned left at Jim's Tavern and made the quick right onto Washington Avenue.

"What are we doing here?" I asked.

"If the niggers won't come to us, we'll have to go to them."

We drove slowly down the street. The houses we passed were no different from those on my own block, but the idea of black people living in them made them seem unfamiliar. Five minutes from home, and I felt like I'd crossed the border into another country. Caravello cut the headlights and pulled over behind the Cherry Street school. He left the engine running.

"There they are," he said.

A bunch of black guys—you could tell from the speed and grace of their game that they were in high school—were running full court on the lot behind the school. It was a weird spectacle at that time of night. Only the two baskets were lit up, one by a spotlight attached to the school, the other, more dimly, by a nearby streetlight. Center court was a patch of darkness.

It was a game of fast breaks. The players would be visible for an instant around one basket, and then they'd scatter abruptly into the shadows, only to emerge seconds later at the other end of the court, already off the ground, arms stretching for a ball we couldn't see.

I was so caught up in the main game that I didn't notice the kid at first. He was about my own age, and he was playing a game of his own. When the real game exploded into light at one end of the court, he'd suddenly appear at the other, driving to the hoop past imaginary opponents, pulling down his own rebounds, always vanishing just before the stampede caught him from behind.

Caravello pummeled the steering wheel and started pressing on the horn, shouting curses into the night. For a second, I thought the car itself was screaming.

"Fuckin' assholes! Chickenshit niggers! Buncha pussies!"

The game stopped. The players near the school and the kid at the far basket turned in our direction. A couple of the bigger guys started toward us, but their movements were confused, hesitant. I yanked Caravello's hand off the steering wheel. The silence came as a jolt.

"Come on," I said. "Let's get outta here."

• • •

The car climbed into the rich hills of West Plains, past stone mansions and big white houses with four or five cars in the double driveways. The air smelled sweet and green.

"Let's get some pussy," Caravello said.

"I have to be home by nine-thirty."

He frowned. "Can't get pussy until ten or so."

"I know. I can't believe my parents still pull this curfew shit on me."

"You think that's bad? My sister's sixteen and my old man still won't let her out of the house on weekends. She just locks herself in her room and cries all the time."

"Jeez."

Caravello took his hand off the wheel and delivered a sharp backhand to my chest. "Ever get any?"

"Any what?"

"Pussy, asshole." He mimicked me. "Duh, any what?"

"Not yet," I said.

"You went with Tina the other night, right?"

"Yeah."

"Are you telling me you didn't get in her pants?"

"Nope."

"Why the fuck not?"

"She wouldn't let me."

Caravello pushed me hard into the passenger door.

"Don't be stupid, Buddy. They all say no, but they don't mean it. It's just something they have to say, so you don't think they're sluts."

"They must mean it sometimes," I said.

Caravello shook his head.

"You better grow up," he told me.

I stared out the window for a while. We drove past Echo Lake. Even at night, you could see that the water was brown and shiny.

McDonald's was on Grand Avenue across from the paper mill. It felt good pulling into the parking lot in the Camaro. Usually I just sat inside the restaurant with friends, sharing fries and writing my name in salt on the tabletop, dreaming of the day when I would have a car.

"Wait for me," I told Caravello. "I gotta take a whizz."

Although the parking lot was packed with cars and kids, the restaurant was nearly empty. My Uncle Ralph was the only customer inside. He sat with his back to me at a table near the window. The dwarf we called Kareem was mopping the floor around my uncle's feet.

The restroom was disgusting. It smelled like somebody had just puked in there. I held my breath and pissed as fast as I could. I flushed the urinal as a favor to Kareem, then went to say hi to my uncle. When I came up behind him he was grinding a cigarette into the overflowing ashtray as though he held a grudge against it. I touched his shoulder.

"Uncle Ralph."

"Buddy, how's it going?" The *National Enquirer* was spread out in front of him like a tablecloth.

"Fine," I said. "What's in the news?"

"Look at this." He pointed with his yellowed fingertip to a headline that read, "Biggest Public Toilet in the Universe!"

"It says here that the Russian astronauts are dumping their excrement directly into outer space. Can you believe it? All these turds just floating around up there?"

"Don't our guys do it too?" I asked.

"No sir. We cart ours home."

"It's really cold up there," I pointed out. "It probably just freezes right up."

"That's not the point," he said.

Kareem looked up suddenly from the floor and fixed the paper cap on his big head.

"The point is to have some respect," he said. His voice was surprisingly deep.

"Amen," said Uncle Ralph.

"Well," I said. "I better get going."

"You sure?" Uncle Ralph asked. "Can I buy you a cup of coffee or something?"

"No thanks. Gotta run."

When I got outside, the car was gone. I figured Caravello had ditched me, and I couldn't really blame him. What could he possibly get out of hanging out with someone who had to be home by nine-thirty? But then the horn honked and I saw him waiting for me on the exit side of the lot, grinning with his metallic teeth. I jogged over to the car feeling like a celebrity.

I opened the passenger door. Tina was in my seat.

"Look who I found," said Caravello.

I started to squeeze into the back seat but Caravello said, "No way. Nobody rides nigger in my car. Tina can sit on your lap."

She sat all the way up by my knees and held onto the dashboard. She waved out the window as we started moving. I turned my head and saw Jane and Donna leaning against a car talking to three blond guys I didn't recognize.

"Those guys are dickheads," Caravello said.

Tina lit a cigarette as we accelerated on Grand. The breeze blew wisps of her hair into my face. I wanted to touch her, but I didn't know where we stood.

"How was the shore?" I asked.

She blew smoke out the window. "Great. Like my tan?" She pulled her shirt away from her shoulder to reveal a tan line as thin and pale as a piece of spaghetti, then twisted her head to look at me. "You know that old guy in McDonald's?"

"Yeah. He's my uncle."

"It's kinda creepy," she said. "It's like he lives in there."

"You have to know him," I said. "His wife died of cancer."

In my mind, I saw Uncle Ralph at the funeral, kissing the flower he dropped in Aunt Dot's grave, my father grabbing him as he stumbled.

"Hey Buddy," Caravello said. "You wanna go home now?" He looked at Tina. "It's past Buddy's bedtime."

"Shut up, Mike," I said.

"Well, it's after nine-thirty."

"Fuck that. I go home when I want to."

Caravello shrugged. "Hey Tina, you go down the shore a lot, don't you?"

"Yeah. We have a summer house in Point Pleasant."

"You got a boyfriend down there?"

She blew a series of quivering smoke rings at the rearview mirror.

"Sort of."

"Is he a lifeguard?"

"No."

"How old is he?"

"Seventeen."

"Do you go all the way?"

She flicked her cigarette out the window.

"You are so queer, Caravello."

For some reason, Tina leaned all the way back, as though I wasn't there. I sank down into the bucket seat beneath her weight. She and Caravello started arguing about the radio station, but I was too absorbed in her body to pay attention. I rested my forehead against the ridge of her spine. She smelled like maple syrup, just the way she had on Friday night.

Tina shifted in my lap. "Am I all right?" she asked.

"You're fine," I told her.

Tina went to Catholic school out of town. When she started showing up at the park that spring, she never talked to me and I couldn't tell if she was stuck up or shy. Now, even after what had happened between us, I still didn't know if she liked me or not.

I closed my eyes and remembered watching her dance. She was wearing a football jersey that hung down past her shorts, number 24. I couldn't take my eyes off the numbers. It was a warm night, but I was wearing an air force shirt that had belonged to my father. I'd recently found four of them inside a trunk in our attic. They were musty from twenty years' storage, but I imagined I could smell faraway places in them, the Philippines, Korea, Japan. During a break in the music, Tina came up to me and tucked a finger in one of my epaulets.

"I love your shirt," she said, her voice sweet with Boone's Farm.

I brushed my fingers against the soft mesh of her jersey.

"I like yours too."

"I'm a little drunk," she whispered.

The band started up again. They were a bunch of gas station attendants who thought they were the Doobie Brothers. Tina grabbed my wrist and pulled.

"Come on and dance."

"I'll watch," I said.

And later, when Tina asked me if I could walk her home, I felt like I was in a dream, it happened so easily.

She lived across town, up in the hills. On the way, we held hands but didn't talk. The world was as still as a photograph. Near her house we took a shortcut through a patch of woods. It was way past my curfew, but we leaned against a tree and started making out. I slid my hand up her shirt in the back and tried to unhook her bra, but I couldn't find anything remotely resembling a hook. After a few minutes of fumbling, I dropped my hands to my sides and collapsed against her, baffled. She reached inside the jersey.

"It snaps in front," she whispered.

I put my hands where hers had been. We stopped kissing and just looked at each other. After a while I pulled up the jersey and burrowed my head beneath the numbers.

Her father was a dentist, and she lived in a big

white house, the kind families live in on television. We kissed good night under a porchlight swarming with moths.

"You want to come in?" she asked. "My parents aren't home."

"Sorry," I said. "I have to go."

She tilted her head; her expression was serious, oddly adult.

"Buddy," she said. "Is this just one of those things?"

"One of what things?"

"You know," she said. "One of those things."

"Yeah," I said. "I guess so."

As soon as she shut the door I started running; my sneakers slapped a steady beat on the sidewalk. The clock in the drugstore window said it was after eleven-thirty, the latest I'd ever been out by myself.

I was panting for air by the time I pushed open the front door. Except for the flickering of the TV, the house was dark. My mother was lying on the couch in her bathrobe, a bunch of balled-up Kleenexes scattered on the carpet below. I waited for her to say something, but she just blew her nose.

I yelped. Caravello had clobbered me on the head with his ring.

"Go on." he commanded. "Tell Tina how scared you were when we went looking for niggers."

"I wasn't scared. You're the one who freaked."

"He shit his pants," Caravello told Tina. "You shoulda seen it."

The weeding implement was on the floor by my feet. I imagined raking it across his face.

"Don't lie," I said.

"You wanna go back?" he sneered. "Or is it past your bedtime?"

"I don't care."

He looked at Tina. "What about you?"

She shrugged.

When we got back to Cherry Street, only the kid was left. He was shooting free throws at a basket near the school. You got the feeling he'd still be there when the sun came up. Tina giggled.

"Let's take his ball," Caravello said.

He whispered the plan. I didn't object, even though I had to do the dirty work. Caravello and Tina were supposed to distract the kid while I snuck up from behind.

I slid out from under Tina and shut the door. The car drove off, and I felt alone and vulnerable, hiding behind a tree near the curb. My head still smarted from Caravello's ring. I had to stamp my feet to get the blood flowing in my legs.

For one rotten moment, I was sure that Caravello had abandoned me, but just then the Camaro swung around the corner and stopped in the street on the other side of the school yard, directly across from me. Caravello honked the horn. His voice carried through the night with awful clarity.

"Hey Tyrone," he shouted. "Is that you?"

The kid stopped shooting. He turned toward the voice with the ball held loosely in the crook of his arm, the way you might hold a book walking home from school. I was surprised to see him wearing long pants on such a muggy night.

He heard my footsteps and whirled around when I was just a few steps away from him. When I saw his frightened face, I screamed. The sound that erupted from my throat was shrill and startled. His eyes got bigger when he heard it.

I drove my shoulder hard into his stomach and took him right off his feet—a perfect open-field tackle. He made just one sound, a gasp of amazement, before his head bounced heavily on the pavement.

The ball was rolling slowly toward the out-of-bounds line. I scooped it up and sprinted for the Camaro. As I ran, I couldn't shake the feeling that I held his head in my hand, clutched tight to my body.

Back in town, we pulled over to the side of the road. Now I was sitting in Tina's lap.

Caravello slapped me five. He was laughing so hard he could barely catch his breath.

"Did you hear that motherfucker scream?" he asked.

"He couldn't help it," I said.

We passed the basketball around as though it were some strange new object, something we'd never seen before. Its surface was worn completely smooth from overuse; it must have been slippery and difficult to play with. Tina stared at the ball for a long time, like someone gazing into the future.

"Spalding," she said finally.

"I better go," I said.

"You want to come swimming at my house?" Tina asked. "My parents aren't home."

"No thanks. I'm late as it is."

"I'll go," Caravello said. "I could use a dip."

Tina poked me in the back. "You sure?"

"Yeah," I said. "It's past my bedtime."

Caravello laughed. I hated him then, in a way that made me feel dumb and helpless.

"Buddy's all right," he announced.


When Caravello dropped me off, I rushed across the lawn without looking back. I didn't want to watch them drive away together. The car peeled out just as I opened the front door.

My parents were both reclining on the couch, heads on opposite ends, legs tangled in the middle. They looked like some giant, two-headed monster of unhappiness.

"Do you know what time it is?" my father asked.

My mother answered for me. "It's twenty after ten. Where were you?"

"Little League, McDonald's, all over. I saw Uncle Ralph in McDonald's. He's worried about the Russians going to the bathroom in outer space."

"Don't change the subject," my father said. "Who's the hotshot that drove you home?"

"No one. I walked."

"Don't lie to us," my mother said sadly.

"Stay out of older kids' cars," my father said. "I'm warning you."

"We heard something about a race riot," my mother said. "We were worried about you."

My parents had recently bought a police radio, so they knew everything that went on in town.

"There wasn't any race riot," I said.

"Where'd you get that basketball?" my father asked.

I'd forgotten that I was holding the ball. I'd also forgotten about the garden tool, which I'd left on the floor of the Camaro. I imagined Tina using it to scratch Caravello's back.

"I found it," I said.

I glared at them, and they frowned back. Somehow I thought that everything that had happened was their fault, not mine. I bounced the ball once on the linoleum hall floor. The sound it made was hard and hollow. I wanted to say something in my own defense, to explain or apologize, but my head felt as empty as the ball in my hand, a round container of air.

# Snowman

Two days ago the snow had swirled and sparkled as it fell, but now it lay hardened on the ground, packed into dirty gray lumps the color of cigarette ash. I was wearing ski mittens and clumsily dribbling a basketball down Grand Avenue while my teammate Neil Duffy strummed air guitar on a snow shovel he'd borrowed from his parents' garage.

We knew we looked stupid. That was the whole point. So it didn't really bother us when this kid in a sheepskin coat zipped by on an English racer, riding against traffic, and shouted, "Assholes!"

"Fuck you!" I shouted back.

Neil's guitar-shovel turned into a machine gun as he whirled and blasted the jerk, who was already receding into the grimy distance, an extra in the movie of our day. Then we laughed, as much at ourselves as at him. Of course we were assholes. Who else would be playing basketball outside in 20-degree weather, just two days after the biggest snowstorm of the year?

It was Neil's idea. Even then, in ninth grade, he had a clear vision of his future. He believed he would someday be a basketball legend, the next great white guy with a deadly jumper, a steady team player who respected the refs and always came through in the clutch. He was preparing for the day when a TV announcer would be able to say: "You know how bad Duffy wanted it? Duffy wanted it so bad he used to go out after blizzards, shovel off the court, and practice until his fingers froze. Then he'd go home, drink a cup of hot cocoa, and head back for more. Now *that's* dedication, Marv."

Basketball didn't mean that much to me. I was a football player and only dabbled in nonviolent sports to keep in shape during the off-season. I was tagging along that morning because I had nothing better to do and liked the idea of participating in Neil's fantasies of fame and glory. He was good enough that you could almost believe they might come true. He went into these streaks sometimes where every shot that spun off his fingertips dropped through the net with a sweet silky whisper. A look came over his face in these moments that was so distant and serene it seemed almost religious. Watching him, you might have thought he heard God calling his name, or one of Charlie's Angels.

We were down by Premier Electric when I felt the hand on my shoulder. It was weird how quietly he'd managed to sneak up. He was straddling the crossbar of his English racer, smiling in a way that might have seemed friendly under other circumstances.

"What did you say back there?"

His voice wasn't angry, but I knew he must have been mad to turn around and ride all the way back. He was a full head taller than me and a couple of years older—at least a junior, maybe even a senior. He looked like a rich kid, with his shaggy blond hair, sleepy eyes, and winter tan, the type that went on ski vacations and spent his summers gazing down at the world from the stilted height of a lifeguard chair. I bounced the ball to show him I wasn't intimidated, crunching the rock salt on the sidewalk.

"Come on," I said, making my voice as reasonable as possible. "You called us assholes."

He smiled a little harder, shaking his head in this slow, arrogant way, like he felt sorry for me. A voice in my head said stay calm. There were two of us and only one of him. And besides, he was wearing that beautiful sheepskin coat. Who would want to fight in a coat like that?

"Just tell me what you said, asshole."

"You heard me."

"I want to hear it again."

I pondered my options. I didn't want to fight, but I didn't want to back down, either. Rules were rules. If someone calls you an asshole for no reason, you definitely have the right to respond.

"I said, 'Fuck you.' "

I felt brave and defiant just then, as though I were standing up for an important principle, but I made one big mistake: I figured he'd have to get off his bike to start something. As a preliminary, I turned to give Neil the basketball.

That was when the psycho lifeguard smashed me in the face. It wasn't the best punch in the world, probably because he threw it flat-footed, but it caught me square in the nose. He wasn't wearing gloves, and it felt like I'd been whacked with a frying pan.

"Hey!" said Neil.

My knees buckled and the world went fuzzy, but I surprised myself by not falling down or dropping the ball. I just stood there, my head vibrating like a gong as he set his bicycle on the ground, then turned and raised his fists. He smiled dreamily, itching to hit me again.

"You've got a pretty smart mouth, don't you?" he asked, as if he hadn't started the whole thing.

At first I tasted just a trickle of blood, but then something happened. There was a rushing noise in my head, followed by a sudden release of pressure. Neil told me later that he'd never seen anything like it, the way the blood just erupted from my nose.

The lifeguard was startled too. His mouth dropped open and his arms fell to his sides. I took advantage of his shock by whipping the basketball at his face. He cringed as it whizzed past his ear; I made my charge. When I slammed into him, we both lost our footing on the icy sidewalk.

We rolled around like wrestlers in the dirty snow. He pounded me ineffectually on the back while I bled profusely on his coat, rubbing my nose with malicious pleasure back and forth across the sheepskin until I was almost drunk from the smell of it, the animal softness. It took him a while to catch on.

"Shit!" he wailed. "My coat!"

"Had enough?" I grunted.

His body went limp. "Yeah."

We untangled ourselves and stood up. He looked down at the dark smears and swirls and splatters on his chest and made this pathetic whimper. He wiped frantically at the stains but they'd already become part of his coat.

"Fuck," he said. "My mom's gonna kill me."

"Serves you right," I told him.

"Yeah," said Neil. He was holding the shovel aloft with both hands, the red scoop trembling in the air like a battle flag. "Serves you right."

The lifeguard looked at me and rolled his eyes, almost like the fight had made us friends. Then he picked up his bike, climbed on, and pedaled off to show his mother what he'd done.

I hadn't seen Andy Zirko for two years when he materialized in the doorway of the Coin Shop and came rushing across the street to see if I was okay. The fight had just ended, and I was sitting on the curb with one hand cupped under my nose to catch the dripping blood, waiting for Neil to return from McDonald's with some napkins.

The Zirko I remembered was as pretty as a girl, with long dark hair that fell like a shadow across half his face, but there was nothing pretty about the kid who squatted down next to me and told me to tilt back my chin. Someone had shaved his head and I could see through the fuzzy stubble to the tiny razor cuts on his scalp. Despite the weather, he wasn't wearing a coat, just a blue and gray flannel shirt with the sleeves ripped off.

In a calm voice, he told me that he'd seen everything—how the big kid had sucker punched me and my friend had let me down. It was disorienting to hear his version of events. I felt like I'd bled my way to at least a draw, but Zirko made it sound terrible, like I'd gotten the shit kicked out of me in a dirty fight.

"You wanna get that guy?" he asked.

"Yeah," I said, not really meaning it.

The word was barely out of my mouth when he jumped up and waved his skinny arm. It seemed to me that he somehow conjured a car out of thin air, a jacked-up Monte Carlo that skidded to a halt in front of us, the back passenger door swinging open just inches from my face. I heard Neil calling my name from down the block as Zirko helped me up and shoved me into the car. We swung a U-turn on the busy street and accelerated toward Cranwood.

"Kid on a bike," Zirko snapped at the driver. He snatched an oily undershirt off the floor and pressed it to my nose.

At the first red light I reached under my butt to remove the hard piece of cardboard I'd mistakenly sat upon, and found myself staring at a pretty little girl with ribbons in her hair and elaborate braces on her arms and legs. The poster child was smiling bravely, floating on a field of blackness, the words "WON'T YOU PLEASE HELP?" blazing above her head in bold white letters. It was a fund-raising card for muscular dystrophy, with rows of tiny slots cut into it for nickels, dimes, and quarters. Most of the slots had coins in them. Zirko yanked it out of my hand and kept on talking.

"I'm telling you," he said. "It was the cheapest shot I ever saw. They were just standing there talking and Pow! I couldn't believe it. He didn't even get off the bike."

The driver turned to me for confirmation. His name was Cockroach, and he was an ugly kid with squinty eyes, a greenish complexion, and one stray tooth that poked across his bottom lip like a fang. Still, I appreciated his concern.

"He started it?"

"Yeah." I pulled the undershirt away from my face. "He called me an asshole so I said, 'Fuck you.' He was bigger, but I didn't care."

Cockroach's friend Danny peered at me over the passenger headrest. He was normal looking, except for a ring of whitehead zits encircling his mouth. I wondered why he didn't just pop them.

"He suckered you?"

"Totally."

"I *saw* it," Zirko reminded them. He took the undershirt out of my hand and dabbed gently at my lips and chin. "His pussy friend just stood there and watched. He should've whacked that faggot across the face with his shovel."

The Monte Carlo's engine throbbed like a bad headache. Cockroach hit the gas a split second before the light changed and we roared through the intersection like cops on a chase. Zirko licked his fingertips and rubbed at the dried blood on my cheek.

"Don't worry," he said. "We'll find the fucker."

• • •

On a hunch of Zirko's we turned off Grand and snaked our way through the developments on the outskirts of Cranwood. He navigated like a psychic, leaning over the front seat and gazing through the windshield with fierce intensity, directing Cockroach on an elaborate series of loops and turns. We scoured the neighborhood for at least fifteen minutes, but the kid was nowhere in sight.

By that point my nose had stopped bleeding and my head had cleared. I thought about Neil and wondered if he'd made it to the playground. I wanted to be there with him, shooting "horse" and working on my behind-the-back dribble. The fight seemed stupid now, a wrong turn in the middle of an otherwise decent Saturday. It would have been fine with me if I never saw the lifeguard again for the rest of my life.

"It's okay," I said. "We might as well forget it."

Zirko was startled by my remark. His head whipped around and he stared at me for a long time, like he was trying to remember who I was. I still couldn't get used to the way he looked with his head shaved. His eyes were huge in his head, but glazed over, lifeless. He touched his index finger to the tip of my nose.

"Don't wimp out on me," he warned.

"I'm not wimping out."

"You said you wanted to get this kid, right?"

He smiled when I nodded. Then he reached under the front seat, pulled out a crowbar, and pressed it into my hand. He didn't let go until my mitten wrapped around it.

Three years earlier, Zirko and I had been teammates for a single season of Pop Warner football. He was two grades ahead of me and only played on the Pee-Wees because he was too small and skinny to compete on the Midget level. I remember laughing with him at practice and pounding on his shoulder pads to loosen up before kickoff. One night a bunch of us went to the St. Agnes carnival and Zirko showed off by swallowing half a dozen live goldfish. He told me afterward that he could feel them thrashing around in his stomach, screaming for their mommies.

The year after that, Zirko made his mark on the world. He got busted for dumping paint in rich people's swimming pools. He'd slip into their yards in the middle of the night with a gallon of Sears Weatherbeater, pry off the top, and drop the open can like a depth charge straight to the bottom of the deep end. He fouled more than twenty pools in one summer and might have ruined a few more if he hadn't developed an urge to release the paint in broad daylight. He told the cops he wanted to watch the colors swirl.

After the arrest, some detectives came to Harding with a search warrant for his locker. From what I heard, they found a blowtorch, a shoebox full of hood ornaments, and a stethoscope that had been reported missing from the nurse's office.

Now, in the car, I felt the need to ask Zirko some serious questions. I wanted to know who had shaved his head, what it looked like when the paint blossomed in the water, and if reform school was as tough as people said. I wanted to ask him what a heart sounded like through a stethoscope, and if he really expected me to hit someone with a crowbar.

I wanted to ask him these things, but it was too late. We turned a corner and there he was: the lifeguard in the sheepskin coat, the jerk who'd called me an asshole.

Cockroach hit the brakes the instant we spotted him. He was about halfway down the block straddling his bike at the edge of a driveway, studying a snowman in someone's front yard. They were only about ten feet apart, and the lifeguard's head was cocked at a funny angle, as though he and the snowman were having a conversation.

He stiffened suddenly and turned in our direction. Somehow, after shooting us only the quickest glance, he seemed to know who we were and what we wanted. He jerked his bike around to make a run for it.

"Get him!" cried Zirko.

In the confusion of the moment, Cockroach

freaked out. He aimed the Monte Carlo straight at the lifeguard and floored it. Our tires whirred on the sandy ice, then caught. We hurtled forward like we'd been blasted out of a cannon.

The lifeguard had quick reflexes. Instead of continuing into the street, he whipped his bike around at the last second and hauled ass down the sidewalk, heading for the intersection we'd just vacated. It was a bold maneuver. Amidst a chorus of groans and curses, we shot right past him.

Cockroach freaked out again and locked up the brakes. We spun out on the slick pavement, sliding sideways for the length of three houses. All four of us screamed at once as the force of the skid pitched us sideways in our seats, then forward, then back again, and we slammed, with an emphatic *thunk*, into a bank of curbside snow. It was a thrilling *Starsky and Hutch* maneuver, a feeling you'd pay money for at an amusement park. No one was hurt, but by the time Cockroach got us backed out and pointed in the right direction, the lifeguard had vanished. Zirko pounded the seat in frustration.

A grim silence prevailed as we resumed our manhunt, prowling methodically along the nearby streets. I pretended to be upset, but deep down I was relieved. I'd lost my stomach for revenge.

"Wait," said Zirko. "Go back."

Cockroach glanced at him in the rearview mirror.

"Back where?"

A thoughtful smile broke the tension on Zirko's face. He shook his head in disbelief, amazed at his own blindness.

"To the snowman," he said.

The way Zirko had it figured, we'd caught the kid in his own driveway. All we had to do was go back and wait. He'd have to show up eventually, and then we'd nab him.

"How do you know?" I asked.

"It's obvious. He was *in* the driveway."

It wasn't obvious to me, but I didn't argue. If it was my driveway, I would've dropped the bike and run like hell for the front door. Still, I didn't want to underestimate Zirko. He seemed to have a sixth sense about tracking people. It amazed me that we'd found the kid in the first place.

He was smart about the surveillance too. There were lots of empty spaces on the street, but he ordered Cockroach to parallel park in a tight spot between a van and a pickup, across the street and a few houses down from the driveway where we'd spotted the lifeguard. He'd have to be right on top of us to know we were there.

Cockroach passed the dead time lighting matches and extinguishing them with a hiss between his spit-moistened fingertips. Danny took a fake nose and glasses out of the glove compartment and sent Cockroach into hysterical giggling fits with imitations of people I didn't recognize. Even with these diversions, though, the air inside the car quickly grew stale with boredom. Cockroach ran out of matches. Somebody farted, and we all rolled down our windows. Danny turned around, staring at Zirko through the vacant frames of his joke glasses.

"Hey Andy, we gonna sit here all day?"

"Yeah," added Cockroach. "I'm starving."

Zirko rubbed his stubble. I thought he was going to snap at them, but he kept his cool.

"Me and Buddy can handle this. Why don't you guys go to McDonald's and come pick us up when you're finished. If you don't see us, honk the horn."

Despite the crowbar in my hand. I felt relaxed and nearly cheerful standing with Zirko in the middle of the windswept street, watching the Monte Carlo fishtail around the corner and out of sight. The worst seemed to be over. I didn't think the lifeguard would be coming back and couldn't see Zirko lasting very long in the cold without a coat.

"Hey Andy," I said. "Want my mittens?"

He blew on his hands and shook his head. We were the only people in sight.

"Come on," he said. "Let's check out that snowman."

Zirko slapped me on the back as we headed across the street. Now that no one was going to be hurt, I could appreciate the morning for the incredible chain of adventures it had been—a fist-fight, a car chase, a near accident, even a stakeout. Neil was going to be jealous when I told him what he'd missed.

"Jesus," said Zirko. "Look at this fucking thing."

We'd passed several snowmen on our search of the neighborhood, but none of them even came close to this one. It was taller than we were and lovingly constructed, the kind of thing you'd definitely stop to admire if you happened to pass it on your bike. It had charcoal eyes, a carrot nose, even a jaunty bowler hat. Its smile was a crescent of bright pennies and its buttons a row of Oreo cookies running down its chest. The most striking feature of all was the snowman's heart: a silver valentine of Hershey's Kisses, inside of which someone had set a snapshot of a Labrador retriever, a pudgy black dog with a sad, intelligent face. The picture was wrapped in plastic, carefully wedged into the snow.

"The dog must have died," I said.

Zirko didn't hear me. He was standing on his tiptoes, reaching for the snowman's bowler hat. He grabbed it, dusted it off, then sailed it like a Frisbee into the street. The hat flew a surprising distance before skipping into the gutter.

"It's like a shrine to the dog," I said, unable to conceal the wonder in my voice.

This time Zirko looked at me, but he still didn't answer. Instead he plucked the carrot right out of the snowman's face and tossed it over his shoulder. Then he removed the charcoals and erased the smile a cent at a time. I didn't get upset until he pulled the photo out of the heart and crushed it in his fist like a candy wrapper.

"Jesus, Andy. That's someone's dog."

He dropped the picture onto the ground, then turned to me with his hand out. I gave him what he wanted.

A snowman doesn't stand much of a chance against a crowbar. When Zirko was finished it was nothing but garbage in the snow, garbage and a handful of pennies.

"Come on," he said. "Let's see if anyone's home."

I wish I could say I followed him up the front steps to talk him out of it or to make sure he didn't do anything crazy, but the truth is, I just followed him. The door was open and we walked right in. The house was quiet and warm, a nice place to enter.

"Chucky," a woman called out. "Is that you?"

Zirko cupped a hand around his mouth.

"Chucky," he sang in a mocking falsetto, "is that you?"

"Who *is* that?" she asked.

As though he were an invited guest, Zirko marched down the hallway toward the source of the voice, a bald skinny kid with bare arms and a snowy crowbar in his hand. I hung back, trying to find my bearings, unable to believe that we'd walked into a stranger's house without knocking or ringing the bell. All at once, everything in the world seemed possible, the worst stuff I could even begin to imagine.

I watched him turn into a doorway and listened to the muffled sounds of a conversation. Maybe a minute passed before Zirko stuck his head out and beckoned me with the crowbar. I shook my head no. His eyes got big; he nodded yes. My wet sneakers squeaked on the floor.

There must have been blood on my face, because the woman gasped when she saw me.

"My God," she said. "Did Chucky do that?"

"Damn right he did," said Zirko.

All I could do was stare. She was about my mother's age, a semi-pretty woman with cloudy eyes and loose brown hair she hadn't bothered to comb. I felt embarrassed for her. It was close to noon and she was still wearing her robe, a dingy pink thing with a sunburst coffee stain on one lapel. We'd caught her in the middle of *Scooby-Doo*. She reached for a glass on the coffee table, then thought better of it and pulled back her hand.

"Are you sure it was Chucky?"

Zirko nodded. "We know Chucky."

She wasn't interested in him. She kept her eyes fixed on me, as though I were the most important person in the world.

"He's a big kid," I told her, spreading my hands to approximate the width of his shoulders. "A big kid in a sheepskin coat. He cursed me out and punched me in the face."

Her shoulders slumped when I said that, and her face just sort of collapsed. She closed her eyes and bit her bottom lip. My feeling toward Zirko at that moment was something approaching awe.

"He's not a bad kid," she told me. "He just doesn't know how to control his temper."

Chucky's mother leaned in close to me at the kitchen table, washing my face with a warm, soapy washcloth. I could smell liquor on her breath and see way down the front of her robe.

"Poor baby," she told me. "You bled a lot."

Zirko snickered, but he looked unhappy and confused. The woman's kindness had stolen his momentum. He pushed his chair away from the table and stood up.

"Come on, Buddy. Let's get outta here."

I tried to get up, but Chucky's mother pressed me back into the chair.

"Just hold on. Chucky should be home any minute. I want him to apologize."

There couldn't have been any blood left, but she kept caressing my face with the washcloth, letting me see her nipples.

"Poor baby," she said again, touching the

washcloth to my ear. I imagined myself in a tub of warm water, Chucky's mother washing me everywhere, her robe open to the waist, whispering as she scrubbed.

Zirko wandered over to the refrigerator and helped himself to some orange juice. He chugged noisily from the carton, letting the yellow liquid dribble down his chin. He was just showing off, trying to get her attention, but she didn't give him the satisfaction.

He put down the OJ and walked over to the sink. There was a nearly empty bottle of vodka right next to the toaster. Zirko unscrewed the cap and took a long swig, grimacing as he swallowed.

Chucky's mother spun to face him, clutching her robe shut with one hand. With her back to me, she no longer looked like a woman to have fantasies about. She was a grown-up, a mother who drank vodka and watched cartoons in her bathrobe on Saturday morning.

"Put that down," she snapped. "What the hell's wrong with you, anyhow?"

Zirko leered at her, tapping the crowbar against his thigh.

"What the hell's wrong with Chucky?"

The woman didn't answer right away. The question seemed to have stunned her. She was a little unsteady on her feet.

"You gedout," she said, indignantly slurring her words, suddenly sounding drunk. "You and your little friend here. Who the hell do you think you are?"

Zirko grinned. He was having fun now. He took another swig of the vodka.

"Maybe we don't want to."

"Come on," I said. "Let's get going."

Zirko shook his head. She threw the wash-cloth down on the table. It landed with a wet slap.

"I said get out."

Zirko shrugged. "I don't feel like it."

The phone was on the wall by the refrigerator. She took a step in that direction. So did he.

"No," he said in a soft, scary voice. "I don't think so."

I can't say how long we remained frozen in place, waiting for someone to make the next move. It was probably only a couple of seconds, but it felt longer. I do know that it was the sound of the opening door that broke our stalemate. All three of us turned at once.

Chucky whimpered in the archway, hugging a grocery bag tight to his chest. He was a big kid in a sheepskin coat, but he wasn't the lifeguard. Not even close.

"Holy shit," said Zirko.

Something was wrong with Chucky. "Water on the brain" was the phrase I'd heard people use. His head was bigger than it was supposed to be, and it swayed like a pendulum as he stood there, as though his neck weren't quite strong enough to hold it steady. He had very little hair and thick glasses that made his eyes seem tiny and faraway.

"Chucky," his mother demanded, "did you hit this boy?"

She pointed at me and shame filled my body like a dense hot liquid. Chucky moved his lips, struggling to form the words. His voice was high and reedlike.

"My snowman," he said. The bag slipped through his arms and burst open at his feet. Lots of soup cans went rolling across the floor.

"Chucky," she said sternly. "Please answer the question."

"My snowman," he repeated, choking back a sob.

I dropped to my knees and began gathering up the cans. Every one of them was exactly the same: Campbell's Chicken and Stars, Chicken and Stars, Chicken and Stars.

"Did you use foul language?"

Zirko knelt beside me to help out. We traded a quick glance, and his eyes were wild with remorse. A horn sounded in the street outside.

We burst out of the house and sprinted across the lawn to the Monte Carlo. Zirko got there first and pulled open the door. We froze in unison.

The lifeguard was in the back seat. He had a rectangle of silver duct tape pressed over his mouth and a hunting knife resting against his throat.

"Look what we found," said Danny. He was holding the knife and grinning like a maniac, still wearing the nose and glasses.

"Yeah," said Cockroach. "We walk into McDonald's, and guess who's there?"

The lifeguard stared at me, pleading with his blue eyes. I felt like I'd stepped outside the boundaries of my own life and would never be allowed back in.

"Please don't hurt him," I said.

Danny's smile disappeared. The lifeguard shut his eyes, bracing himself for pain. I saw myself at the supper table with my parents, trying to explain my innocence.

"Let him go," said Zirko.

The lifeguard opened his eyes. Danny squinted through the fake glasses.

"Really?"

Zirko nodded. There was an odd look on his face, like he was disgusted by his own decision.

Danny withdrew the knife. Without removing the tape from his mouth, the lifeguard got out of the car and stood politely by the curb in his blood-stained coat.

I watched him out the back window as we drove away. He didn't move a muscle, and I couldn't help thinking how sorry he must have been for what he called me.

• • •

Neil was still at the playground when Cockroach dropped me off. He didn't bother to acknowledge me as I trudged across the snowy field to join him.

He didn't seem to be having much fun. He'd shoveled off half a court, but it was really too cold to be shooting hoops. His hands were pink and stiff, nearly frozen.

I grabbed a rebound and threw him a bounce pass. His baseline jumper was short; the whole backboard shivered when the ball struck the rim. I shot a layup with my mitten, then fed him another pass. He caught the ball and held it.

"That was Zirko, wasn't it?"

"Yeah."

"I thought he was in reform school."

"I guess they let him out."

"Did you find the kid?"

"No," I lied.

Neil's next shot was an air ball, way too long. It arced past the basket, right into my hands.

"I wanted to hit him," he said, "but I couldn't do it."

"It's okay. I bled all over his coat."

Neil smiled. "That was pretty cool."

He tried to spin the ball Globetrotter-style on his fingertip, but it slid right off.

"Your ball sucks," he told me.

"It's not mine. I stole it from a black kid."

"Why'd you do that?"

I shrugged. "Mike Caravello sort of made me."

Neil made a face and put up another air ball. He missed his next shot and the one after that. I know I'm wrong, but in my memory it seems like he lost his touch forever on that freezing afternoon. For all his talent, he never made it to national television; he never even made the varsity team at Harding. He's a landscaper now. When I'm home in Darwin I see him driving through town sometimes, towing a trailer full of lawn mowers.

I never became the football hero I expected to be either. I lasted just one more season, got tired of it, and drifted on to other things. I never saw the lifeguard again, or Danny, or Chucky, or his mother. I did run into Cockroach at a bar once. He was with a girl and asked me to please call him Frank. As for Zirko, there's not a lot to tell. He dropped out of high school and joined the navy, floating far away from Darwin.

But all that was the future, and the future didn't exist for Neil and me as we tried to salvage the remainder of that freezing Saturday with a game of one on one. The score was 5–3, his favor, when we stopped for a breather at the top of the key.

"Hey Neil," I said, "do you have a dog?"

"Yeah. German shepherd."

"Boy or girl?"

"Girl. Sheba."

I bounced the ball a couple of times, searching for a way to phrase my next question. There was a big knot inside of me I was hoping to untangle.

"Do you like her? Would you be really sad if she died?"

His gaze traveled up from the ball to my face. He looked hurt.

"She's only seven."

His answer must have satisfied me. I tossed him the ball.

"Check," he said, bouncing it right back.

I gave a pump fake and took it to the hoop.

# Forgiveness

**F**ifteen minutes before the opening kickoff of our '76 state championship game, Rocky DeLucca quit the football team. Harding High never forgave him. Rocky was not only starting halfback and varsity co-captain, he was also president of the Student Council, which voted to impeach him the following week. A lot of people stopped talking to him. Nasty messages were scrawled on his locker. But Rocky barely noticed. All he wanted to talk about was love.

"You know what it's like?" he told me. "It's like the whole world's in black and white, but Wendy and I are in color. I don't know how else to explain it."

In the weeks before Rocky's downfall, I had gotten to know him pretty well. We were the only two football players on the Student Council, and he had gone out of his way to be my friend even though I was nobody special, just a sophomore benchwarmer. He gave me a ride home a couple of nights in September when practice ran late; gradually it turned into a regular thing.

Rocky was a short muscular guy with a big Italian Afro, olive skin, and a dazzling smile. On Fridays during the season, when football players were required to wear their game jerseys to school, he wore his under a corduroy blazer with patches on the sleeves. He was so cool that it took me a while to admit to myself that he was also a little strange. As popular as he was, he didn't have a girlfriend or a group of guys he hung out with; as far as I could tell he spent his nights at home. He had a cassette player in his car, but only one tape—"I Got a Name" by Jim Croce—which he played over and over, despite my protests. I gathered from remarks he made that he had experienced Croce's death as a personal tragedy.

One rainy night in October he turned to me and said, "You ever get the feeling that everything's a dream?"

"Only when I'm sleeping," I said.

He ignored me. "Sometimes, right in the middle of the most ordinary situations, I get this weird humming noise in my head and everything starts glowing a little around the edges. It happens a lot during football games. I feel like I'm the only person alive, and everyone else is just a figment of my imagination."

"Jeez," I said. "Maybe it's time for a new helmet."

Another night, after a grueling practice, he asked me if I liked football. Actually, I was having a miserable season. I hated sitting on the bench. But Rocky was team captain so I said, "Are you kidding? I love it."

He shook his head. "I don't know what's wrong with me. I just can't get excited about it this year."

I was stunned. Our team was undefeated, ranked fifth in the county, ahead of many larger schools. Rocky was playing well.

"What don't you like about it?"

"The mind control. I listen to the coaches for five minutes, and the word 'bullshit' starts running through my head like a mantra."

"A what?"

"A mantra," he said. "A word you meditate on."

Before the impeachment, Rocky's main presidential duty was to say the Pledge of Allegiance over the school PA every morning. You could tell from his voice that he wasn't too thrilled about it. At Harding, it was considered uncool to get too worked up about saluting the flag. The unwritten rule was that you had to stand up, but were not required to put your hand over your heart or actually say the words.

While the rest of my homeroom slouched and mumbled along with Rocky, Wendy Edwards remained seated and went on with her reading. Wendy was a fanatical reader; it was hard to tell if she was making a statement or was simply oblivious to the ritual. But she wasn't a troublemaker, so Mrs. Glowacki left her alone.

On the Wednesday before the state championship game, Coach Whalen was walking in the hall when Rocky asked everyone to please rise. Whalen didn't want to miss the Pledge of Allegiance, so he stepped into the nearest room, which happened to be ours, and slapped his hand smartly against his chest.

Coach Whalen was a school legend. In only three years, he had taken a losing team at a second-rate school and turned it into a football powerhouse. He was handsome and charismatic, a Vietnam vet with chiseled features and shaggy, wheat-colored hair (a lot of girls thought he looked like Robert Redford). The class responded to his presence. We stood up straighter and pledged allegiance with more fervor than usual.

Only Wendy seemed unaware of our visitor. She was sitting Indian-style in her chair, holding a paperback close to her nose and twirling a strand of hair around her finger. I saw Coach Whalen's head snap in her direction, watched the blood travel up his thick neck into his face, like mercury rising in a thermometer. When the class sat down, he strode past Mrs. Glowacki's desk and tapped Wendy on the shoulder.

"What's the matter?" he asked, a little too politely. "Are you tired?"

Wendy gave him a blank look, then shook her head. Whalen's hands curled into fists, then slowly relaxed. He looked like he wanted to spit.

"Get up," he said, "and march your butt down to Mr. Wyznewski before I lose my temper."

Later that day, word spread that Mr. Wyznewski had given her two weeks' detention for sitting through the Pledge of Allegiance. Rocky was fascinated by the news.

"Do you know her?"

"Yeah," I said. "We grew up together."

"What's she like?"

"Not bad. Pretty nice tits."

He gave me a look, so I started over.

"I mean she's smart," I said. "But kind of spooky."

Wendy and I were in first grade when her brother died of leukemia. He was only nine years old. A minister took her out of school, and the next day we made condolence cards with crayons and construction paper. Mine had a picture of a little boy floating above a house.

"I'm sorry about Mike," it said.

Wendy lived around the corner from me. Her

dog, Angel, was a goofy-looking mutt, all black except for three white paws. He trotted around our neighborhood at a brisk clip, as though he were late for an appointment, but would always stop and permit his ears to be scratched by anyone who knew his name. I didn't have a dog, so I stopped him every chance I got; we were friends. But one day when I was in sixth grade, after years of mutual affection, Angel bit me for no reason. He sank his fangs into the meat of my hand, then hustled off with his tail wrapped tightly between his legs.

The pain wasn't terrible; it must have been the betrayal that made me so furious. I ran home and showed my mother the torn flesh, expecting her to share my outrage. But she didn't say anything as she cleaned the wound.

"Aren't you going to call?" I demanded.

"I don't know, Buddy. I hate to bother Jeanette."

"Angel's dangerous, Ma. What if he bites some little kid?"

My mother called, but she was a bit too friendly for my taste. After about five minutes of small talk she finally got around to mentioning that I'd had a run-in with Angel.

"Run-in?" I said, loud enough for Mrs. Edwards to hear. "He almost took my hand off."

My mother glared at me, but kept talking in

her sugary voice. I could tell she was mad at me when she hung up.

"Hey," I said. "Angel bit me. I didn't bite him."

"Buddy, Mrs. Edwards has more important things to worry about than Angel."

"Yeah? Like what?"

"Like her husband's dying," my mother said softly. "That's what."

A couple of weeks later, when my hand was healed, Wendy burst into tears in the middle of social studies. Mr. Wallace asked her what was wrong.

"My dog got put to sleep," she said. "I miss him."

"I'm sorry," said Mr. Wallace. "Was he old and tired?"

Wendy sniffled and shook her head. I felt sick to my stomach.

"No," she said. "He bit people."

Not long after Angel, her father died. Wendy was only out of school for a week, but she looked different when she came back. She kept her eyes wide open all the time, like she'd forgotten how to blink.

Despite the detention, Wendy refused to stand on Thursday. She sat with her hands folded and stared straight ahead at the empty blackboard. Mrs. Glowacki spoke to her at the end of homeroom, but whatever she said, it didn't work. Wendy remained seated again on Friday, even though Coach Whalen and Mr. Wyznewski were watching her from the doorway. She didn't even wait for them to speak. As soon as the pledge ended, she stood up and followed them out the door. She was suspended for three days.

Whalen would have busted her on Thursday, but he'd had a more pressing problem to deal with. Randy Dudley, our all-county middle linebacker, had gotten arrested. With just two days to go before the big game, his timing couldn't have been worse.

Randy was a great player but a frightening person. On Wednesday morning his girlfriend, Janet Lorenzo, had come to school with a black eye. No one had to ask her where she got it. That night, Randy got drunk and went to her house to apologize, but Janet's father wouldn't let him in. Heartbroken, Randy took a crowbar to the windshield of Mr. Lorenzo's Oldsmobile, then led the cops on a high-speed chase through three towns that ended when he missed a turn and flattened a mailbox.

As far as Whalen was concerned, drunk driving was the most serious charge. Team training rules prohibited smoking, drinking, and drugs during the season. The policy was simple: get caught and you were gone. Two scrubs had already been kicked off the team when they made the mistake of buying a six-pack in a bar where a couple of coaches happened to be drinking.

At Thursday's practice, Whalen gave us the verdict: Randy wouldn't be allowed to play on Saturday.

Rocky was glad to see Randy go. He said that if we couldn't win without a guy like that, we didn't deserve to be state champs. I disagreed. If we beat Pine Ridge, the Booster Club was going to buy us expensive championship jackets with leather sleeves and our names written over the heart. I believed that the jacket would redeem the whole wasted season, and I didn't want to lose it at the last minute, just because Randy Dudley rammed his Skylark into a mailbox.

The cheerleaders kicked off Friday's pep rally with a foot-stomping routine. Their saddle shoes raised a thunderous din in the big drafty gymnasium. They clapped their hands and sang to the crowd; the crowd clapped and sang back:

> We are Harding
> Mighty, mighty Harding!

They ended with their most famous cheer. They turned their backs to the bleachers, bent over, and flipped up their pleated skirts. Sitting with my teammates on the gym floor, all I could see was a row of red smiling faces, but I knew that they had each ironed a yellow letter on their blue panties, so their butts together spelled "GO HARDING!" The crowd loved it.

The cheerleaders scampered off the court. Coach Whalen took the microphone. He said that he had planned on talking about the game, but something else was on his mind. Something more important than football. He pointed to the American flag hanging on the wall next to the banners commemorating our conference championships in 1974 and '75.

"When I was in Vietnam," he said, "there were people at home, not much older than you, who got their kicks out of spitting on that flag. I guess they thought it was fun. But let me tell you something: for those of us who were serving our country, it wasn't a helluva lotta fun."

He didn't sound angry. His voice was so calm, he could have been lecturing us about the rules of paddleball.

"I don't know," he said. "I thought I'd put it all behind me. I thought it was ancient history. But something happened this week in this school that brought it all back to me. I've been thinking about my friends again. The ones who came home in bags. The ones who were buried in coffins with that flag draped on top."

A hush came over the gym. Whalen looked up, as though his speech were written on the ceiling.

"A lot of brave men died in that war. And they didn't just die of bullets and shrapnel. They died of broken hearts. It broke their hearts to know that people at home were rooting for the other team. Just remember one thing: we didn't lose that war because the other guys were better. We lost because the people at home weren't behind us one hundred percent."

Whalen took a handkerchief out of his back pocket and wiped his forehead. He glanced over his shoulder at the team sitting behind him.

"The players on this football team are about to take part in the most important game of their lives. They're ready. They've made the sacrifices. They've paid the price. But you know what? It doesn't matter how good we are. If the students of this school aren't behind us a hundred percent, we don't stand a chance. So let me ask you one very important question: Are you with us?"

A roar rose from the bleachers. Whalen cupped his hand around his ear. "That doesn't sound like a hundred percent to me."

This time the gym just exploded. People clapped, screamed, and stamped their feet. The cheerleaders shook their pompoms; someone blew an airhorn. The noise wouldn't stop. It sounded like a Zeppelin show at the Garden.

"What did you think of that speech today?" Rocky asked.

We were sitting in Bella Roma Pizza after the Friday night team meeting, where we had watched a depressing film of Pine Ridge's last game. They had this great 200-pound fullback, and I didn't see how we were going to stop him without Randy Dudley.

"I thought it was pretty good," I said.

He brushed imaginary crumbs off the tabletop.

"It was bullshit."

"Why?"

"Come on," he said. "What does Vietnam have to do with anything?"

"He was there. If you fought in a war, I bet you'd talk about it."

The owner's daughter came out with our slices. Her family had only been in America for about a year, but she was already wearing green eye shadow and a Lynyrd Skynyrd T-shirt.

"My brother was there," Rocky said. "He doesn't talk about it."

"I didn't know you had a brother."

"He's older."

"What's he do?"

Rocky tipped his slice to let the grease drip onto his paper plate. "I keep telling him he should go on *Jeopardy*, but he says it's rigged."

It was almost curfew time when we got back to the car. Team members were supposed to be home by nine on game nights, in bed by ten. Rocky slipped the key in the ignition.

"You think Wendy's home?"

"Now?"

"It's not even nine o'clock."

"What about the curfew?" I asked.

He started the engine. "What about it?"

Wendy and her mother lived in a big run-down house with crumbling front steps and a weedy lawn. The neighbors (my parents included) considered it an eyesore, but they understood it more as a sign of misfortune than neglect. Wendy came to the door holding a book, wearing a pair of rumpled men's pajamas, white with blue stripes. Her hair, which she usually wore in a pony tail, hung loosely around her shoulders. She gave me a look that most people reserve for vacuum cleaner salesmen and Jehovah's Witnesses.

"What do *you* want?" she asked.

"My friend wants to meet you," I said.

Rocky stepped forward and introduced himself. He held out his hand. Wendy hesitated, then reached out and shook.

"We're going for a ride," Rocky said. "Would you like to come?"

"Where are you going?"

"Nowhere special."

Wendy's brow wrinkled. She looked down at her baggy pajamas.

"I'll have to change."

Rocky smiled; it was like a gift he gave to certain people. He had smiled at me in exactly the same way when he had decided to be my friend.

"Take your time," he told her.

We waited in the living room. Rocky examined the bookshelves while I studied the pictures on the mantelpiece. There was an old black and white photo of Mike pulling Wendy in a wagon, Angel trotting behind. All three of them wore birthday hats, the pointy kind with elastic chinstraps.

As soon as we got in the car, Rocky and Wendy began to talk nonstop. About the Pledge of Allegiance, about the possibility of ever *really* knowing someone, about places in the world they'd like to visit. Then they got onto religion. I was sitting by myself in the back seat, listening to the song "Operator." I'd heard it a hundred times, but had never realized how sad it was, that when Jim Croce said there was something in his eyes, he was talking about tears.

"If God loves everyone," Wendy said, "then what's the point?"

"Don't even try to figure it out," Rocky told her. "Religion's just another form of mind control."

We were heading west on Route 22. Neon martini glasses and bowling pins flashed in the roadside darkness. I loved the feeling of driving at night, the edgy combination of security and adventure. You were safe; anything could happen.

"What about you, Buddy?" Rocky asked.

"Do you believe in God?"

"Sure. Somebody created the world."

"Not necessarily," Wendy said. "It could just be this big chemical accident."

"Yeah, right," I said.

Rocky turned off the highway onto a narrow two-lane road. We passed a series of signs for the VA Hospital, and finally the hospital itself, this bright hulking complex in the middle of nowhere.

"When my brother was shot," Rocky said, "my mother felt the pain. We were sitting at the kitchen table eating supper and all of a sudden she screamed and grabbed her shoulder. She almost fell off her chair. 'My God,' she said. 'Chuck's been hit.' "

"Come on," I said. "That didn't happen."

"I believe you," Wendy told him. "A year after my father died, I saw him on *Truth or Consequences*. He was sitting in the studio audience, waving at the camera. And it wasn't just someone who looked like him, either. He was wearing a sweater I gave him for Christmas."

"Jesus," Rocky whispered.

My scalp tightened. If anyone else had told me these stories, I would have laughed at them. But Rocky and Wendy were different. Things had happened to them that hadn't happened to me. I had the awful feeling they were telling the truth.

The car labored uphill through Watchung Reservation, past the water tower I'd climbed a long time ago with my cub scout den. You could see the Manhattan skyline from the observation deck, which had been closed for a couple of years now, ever since a kid had thrown himself off, an honor student. We followed the bumpy road until it petered out in a gravel parking area not far from Surprise Lake.

We walked in single file down a moonlit path. The night air was cold and still. We stood together on the shore and stared at the quivering silver surface of the lake. I picked up a rock and threw it in the water.

Saturday was crisp and sunny, a perfect day for football. Rocky was supposed to pick me up at ten, but he didn't show up until quarter after. He was grinning like an idiot, his hair still wet from the shower.

"What's with you?" I asked.

He closed his eyes, shook his head in slow motion, the way my father sometimes did in the middle of an especially good meal.

"It happened, Buddy. I fell in love."

"Gimme a break."

"I'm serious," he said. "Wendy's an amazing person."

He turned right instead of left on West Street, just so he could circle past Wendy's house.

"There she is," he said.

Incredibly, she was standing on the front

porch in her pajamas, holding a coffee mug. Rocky honked as we drove by; Wendy smiled and waved. I should have been happy for him, but I was vaguely annoyed. I wanted to tell him that he could do better than Wendy, that there were lots of normal, pretty girls who would have gone out with him in a minute.

"You just met," I said. "You hardly know her."

"After you went home, we stayed up talking until three in the morning. I feel like I've known her all my life."

"Three in the morning? Christ, Rock. I hope you're ready for this game."

"I'm ready." His voice was quiet and confident.

"You really think we can win without Randy?"

"Absolutely."

The rest of the team wasn't so sure. The atmosphere in the locker room was almost unbearably tense. Starters were lined up three and four deep in front of the bathroom stalls, waiting for a chance to puke up their butterflies. Other guys were sitting half-dressed in front of their lockers, mumbling to themselves. My stomach was in a complicated knot.

We took the field for about a half-hour of warm-ups, then returned to the locker room. While Coach Whalen gave the pep talk, one of his assistants, Coach Bielski, wandered through the room, smearing black goop under the eyes of the important players. My heart raced as he approached; I had the strange feeling that today, for the first time, he was going to reach down and blacken my eyes, initiating me with that simple gesture into the inner circle of the team. But he just walked on by, as usual.

On paper, Whalen said, Pine Ridge had all the advantages. They were bigger, faster, more experienced. They had nicer uniforms and a better marching band. Their parents made more money than ours did. But that was just on paper, and paper didn't win football games. Heart did. And the rich boys from Pine Ridge didn't have the heart to beat us, especially not on our home field. As far as we were concerned, they were foreign invaders, and we were to treat them accordingly. From the opening kickoff to the final whistle, it was our job to make them suffer, to make them good and sorry they'd ever heard of Warren G. Harding Regional High School. Because tonight, when it was all over, they were just going to be a bunch of beat-up rich kids. We were going to be State Champions. He paused to let that sink in, then led us in our customary pre-game prayer.

I always felt close to my teammates when we prayed, all of us on one knee, heads bowed, listening to Whalen ask God to prevent serious injuries and grant us the strength and wisdom to prevail, amen. When the prayer was over, he said something that surprised me.

"Men," he said. "What does Jesus Christ stand for?"

No one answered.

"Come on," he coaxed. "Don't be afraid."

"God?" someone suggested.

"Miracles?"

"Eternal life?"

"Those are good answers," he said. "But Jesus also stands for something else. He stands for forgiveness."

You didn't have to be a genius to see what was happening. Whalen motioned toward the corridor, and Randy Dudley stepped into the room. The tension in the air dissolved like smoke. There he was, Big Number 56, rescued from oblivion. I felt like I had just witnessed a neat magic trick, like Whalen had pulled Randy out of a hat.

"Men," he said. "Randy has something to tell us."

Randy tried to keep a straight face as he spoke. It wasn't easy. "I'm sorry I let the team down," he told us. "What I did was wrong."

Whalen draped his arm around Randy's shoulder pads. A smile blossomed on his normally stern face.

"What do you say, men? Will we let bygones be bygones?"

My head was nodding along with the others when I heard the voice.

"This is bullshit."

Whalen's head jerked to one side, as though he'd been slapped.

"Who said that?"

Rocky stood up. He looked fierce with the black war paint underlining his dark eyes.

"I did."

Whalen stayed calm. He glanced around the room to make sure he didn't have a mutiny on his hands. Since we had a difference of opinion, he said, our only alternative was to take a vote on whether or not Randy should be forgiven.

Rocky was my friend, but even so, there wasn't much of a choice. I wanted to be a state champ. I wanted to stay on the right side of the coaches. And I wanted that jacket with my name on it. The idea of betrayal didn't even enter into my calculations. When the time came I made sure not to look at Rocky. I just raised my hand along with everyone else and voted yes, in favor of forgiveness.

The game itself turned out to be pretty boring. The score was tied 0-0 until late in the fourth quarter, when Rocky's replacement, a slippery junior named Tim LeMaster, ran forty yards for what turned out to be the winning touchdown. When the game ended Coach Whalen cried and led us on a victory parade through the streets of Springdale. Hundreds of people lined the route, cheering us on.

There was a wild celebration that night at Eileen Murphy's. People were drinking grain alcohol mixed with Kool-Aid. The music was louder, the dancing crazier than usual. It was like that picture from the end of World War II: you could grab any girl you wanted and kiss her on the lips. I saw Randy Dudley and Janet Lorenzo making out on the couch. He had his hand inside her sweater. Her black eye had almost healed. In a day or two, I thought, no one would even remember it.

I left around ten and walked across town to Rocky's house. His brother, Chuck, answered the door. The resemblance was striking, even though Chuck had straight hair and a beard streaked with gray. I tried not to stare at the empty shirt sleeve tucked neatly into the pocket of his jeans.

"Is Rocky home?"

Chuck shook his head. "He's at his girl-friend's."

I headed back to my own neighborhood. Wendy's house was dark, but I saw with relief that Rocky's station wagon was parked out front. I climbed the steps, took a deep breath, and rang the bell, already rehearsing my apology. The door creaked open. Wendy put her finger to her lips before I could speak.

"We're having a seance," she whispered.

"I didn't mean to interrupt," I said.

"Don't be silly. We were hoping you'd come."

A single candle was burning in the middle of the kitchen table. Shadows trembled on Rocky's face as he watched me walk past the refrigerator and sit down across from him. I was nervous at first. I had never taken part in a seance and wasn't sure about the procedure.

It's not that complicated. You hold hands. No one makes a sound. You try not to smile.

# A Bill Floyd
# Xmas

**E**very December, my father and I went up to the attic and carried down a big cardboard box with the words "NONFLAMMABLE XMAS TREE" printed on all four sides. We opened the box in the living room and removed the paper bags stacked inside. The bags were numbered and contained branches made of green bristle and twisted wire. Off the tree, they looked like something you would use to clean a toilet.

It was easy to build the tree. First we screwed two green dowels together to make a trunk, then stood the trunk upright in a red metal stand. Starting from the bottom and working up, we inserted branch stems into holes drilled in the trunk. After my father set the tree's cactus-shaped crown in place, my mother joined us to hang the ornaments and string the tinsel garlands. We wrapped a glittery cloth around the base, then fastened a blinking angel to the top branch. When we were through, it was hard to believe our tree had come in a box.

This tradition lasted until 1977, my junior year of high school, when I came home from the deli where I worked and found an immense new tree in the living room. It was bare of ornaments and powerfully sleek, like a green rocket about to blast off through the ceiling. A short distance away, my father sat in his usual spot on the couch, reading the newspaper.

"You could have waited for me," I said. "I would have helped you put it together."

He brought the paper slowly away from his face. It took a few seconds for my words to register.

"Nothing to help with." He got up from the couch. My father wasn't a small man, but he looked small standing next to the tree. He tugged on a branch to demonstrate that it wouldn't detach. "Nope," he said. "This one's a unit."

"Where'd you get it?"

"Bill Floyd."

"Why'd Bill Floyd give you a Christmas tree?"

"His mother passed away this summer. He says he's not in the mood for Christmas." My father shrugged. "I jumped when he made the offer."

Just then my mother came down the stairs, a stack of ornament boxes loaded up to her chin. I took half of them off her hands.

115

"Hi, Buddy," she said, examining my eyes for signs of drug abuse. "How was work?"

"Slow. So how do you like the new tree?"

"Well," she said, kneeling to set down the boxes, "it sure is bigger than the old one."

After supper I headed out to band practice, my regular destination on Tuesday and Thursday evenings. I played lead guitar in a band called Rockhead. Music had filled the void in my life after I quit the football team at the beginning of my junior year. The band seemed to offer all the rewards of football—teamwork, dedication, the promise of glory—without any of the drawbacks, such as coaches, pain, and smelly uniforms.

Halfway down the block from Ed Kelso's house, I could already hear music blasting from the basement. I let myself in through the side door and headed downstairs, the wooden steps throbbing beneath my feet. Ed and Dirk nodded when they saw me, but kept on jamming. They sounded hot together, so hot I was grateful just to be present. They were real musicians, playing on a level I could only dream about. I knew a few fast licks, but I was just a beginner. I didn't even have my own amp.

My friend Ed was the brains behind the band. He was a great rhythm guitarist and the only singer around who could hit all the high notes in a Zeppelin song. He was also overweight and extremely shy, with a bad habit of falling desperately in love with girls he'd never met, and becoming furious when they acted like he didn't exist. To cheer himself up, he would get drunk and break some windows. It was an exhausting cycle.

Dirk was a wildman drummer, the only one of us who really looked like a rocker. He had stringy blond hair and a wardrobe of patched jeans and loud dashikis. He claimed to have been stoned since 1974, and although I'd only known him for a few months, I had no reason to doubt his word. He lived in Cranwood and knew Ed from the Minutemen Drum & Bugle Corps. I couldn't imagine Dirk in a lame outfit like that, with tri-corner hats and personalized windbreakers, but he assured me it was totally cool—the girls in the piccolo section really knew how to party.

We only knew eight songs, so practice didn't last very long. When it was over, we made our usual run to the ice cream store in Cranwood where Dirk's girlfriend worked. It was only eight-thirty when we arrived, but Sally flipped the sign on the front window from Open to Closed and locked the door behind us.

"Doesn't matter," she said. "All they can do is fire me."

We followed her into the back room. Even at work, Sally dressed in Deadhead clothes: tie-dyed sweatshirt, peasant skirt with long johns underneath, work boots with orange laces. She had long straight hair and bluejay-feather earrings that dangled past her shoulders. When she reached for the radio on top of the soft-serve machine, she stood on tiptoes with one leg curved behind her, like a ballerina.

Dirk rolled some joints on a stainless steel table cluttered with stacks of cups, cones, and cake boxes. While we smoked, I told them about my family's new Christmas tree. Dirk and Sally weren't familiar with Bill Floyd, so I had to explain that he worked with my father and was known around town as "Toupee Ray" because of his hairpiece.

"It looks like there's an animal on his head," Ed said. "A squirrel parted on the side."

Sally took a hit off the roach and spoke with her breath held in. "So why do you have his tree?"

"His mother died. He didn't want it anymore."

Dirk scratched his head. He looked like he was taking a hard test. "So wait a minute. How old is this guy?"

"I'm not sure. Maybe like fifty."

"This guy is fifty years old and living with his mother?"

Ed laughed. His eyes had narrowed to the size of dime slits. "His mother's dead, asshole."

"But when she was alive he lived with her, right?"

"Right," I said.

"So why'd he wear a toupee?" Dirk seemed

baffled by his own question.

Ed tapped on his skull. "Are you brain-damaged, man?"

"You guys are stoned," I said.

Sally banged on the table with an ice cream scoop, like a judge calling for order.

"I just made a tub of Rocky Road. Anybody want some?"

When I got home, Bill Floyd was in the living room with my parents. The TV was going, but no one was watching it. Bill Floyd had the recliner swiveled to face my mother, who was sitting in an easy chair that had been moved almost into the hallway to make room for the tree. My father was out cold on the couch, snoring like a cartoon character.

My mother smiled at me. "Guess what? Mr. Floyd baked us some Christmas cookies." She had a special tone of voice that she only used when we had company. It made the simplest fact sound like cause for celebration.

"That's right," he said. "They're in the kitchen."

I mumbled a few syllables and hurried into the kitchen, relieved to find such an easy way out of small talk. I hadn't expected to see Bill Floyd, and all I could think of was Ed's crack about his toupee looking like a squirrel.

The cookies were green and shaped more or

less like wreaths. Each one was studded with a single bright red candy. Bill Floyd appeared in the doorway and asked how I liked them.

"Terrific," I said. "Still nice and chewy."

"My mother's recipe," he told me. "It's not Christmas without them."

He said good night, and I heard the front door close. My mother came into the kitchen with three empty glasses.

"Whew," she said. "I thought he'd never leave. Your father fell asleep an hour ago. I was trying to watch the Andy Williams special, but he talked so much I hardly caught a second of it."

I could see she was annoyed. My mother had a big crush on Andy Williams and often referred to him as her "boyfriend." I put another cookie in my mouth and spoke through the crumbs. "So what did he talk about?"

She picked up a sponge and started scrubbing at a spot on the Formica countertop.

"He talked about his mother," she said. "He misses her."

I had to work at the deli on Christmas Eve. I made a few sandwiches at lunchtime, then killed an hour with chores, cleaning the slicer and straightening the snack cakes. After that there was nothing to do but wait for an occasional customer to drift in for cigarettes or milk. I passed the time warming my hands over the open oven door while old man

Freund napped, chin in hand, at his little table in the back.

Near closing time he came back to life and joined me at the oven. We stood close together in our soiled aprons, washing our hands in the hot, rising air. Mr. Freund squinted suspiciously at the Schickhaus clock, which had hot dogs for hands.

"Where did the day go?" he asked.

I shrugged. "It just went."

At five o'clock I hung up my apron and headed outside to do my Christmas shopping. I had to hurry, because I'd promised my mother that I'd come straight home from work to help her with the luminaria. This was a fancy word for candles anchored in sand at the bottom of hamburger take-out bags. A neighborhood committee had enlisted our entire street to line the sidewalks with them on Christmas Eve.

Medi-Mart was delirious with last-minute shoppers. The shelves looked looted; even the Muzak seemed hectic. I bought my father a carton of cancer sticks, a Pepperoni and Assorted Cheeses Gift Pack, and a paperback about Pearl Harbor. I got my mother a battery-operated minivacuum and a small bottle of perfume. I also picked up a glossy greeting card: "A Christmas Prayer for You, Mother and Dad."

Only two registers were open, and I got on the slow line. Three people ahead of me, this woman in a kerchief started an argument about the price of a jigsaw puzzle that had two stickers on it. She insisted on speaking to the manager, who seemed mysteriously difficult to locate. By that time, it was too late for me to change lines.

The bag of presents bounced against my thigh as I jogged home through the darkness. It was nearly six o'clock, zero hour for the candles. We'd never get them set up in time. Once again, through no fault of my own, I'd let my mother down.

But when I turned the corner of our street, I saw that the bags were already out, neatly arranged along both borders of the sidewalk. As I approached the house, I could barely make out the outlines of two people standing in the driveway.

"Thanks a lot," my mother said.

"Sorry. The mall was a madhouse."

"I was lucky," she said. "Mr. Floyd saved my life."

Bill Floyd waved a candle to ward off her praise. I glared at him, but he didn't seem to notice. "I was just passing by," he explained in a cheery voice. "Glad to be of assistance."

Our neighbors began coming out of their houses, hands full of little white bags. Friendly greetings traveled up and down the block through the freezing air. The church bells started ringing and we lit the candles. Locust Street was suddenly aglow with lines of soft light that stretched as far as you could see in both directions.

•   •   •

At the supper table, my father asked if I was going to midnight mass. It was a family tradition: he and I went to church on Christmas Eve while my mother, the only one of us who believed in God, stayed home and wrapped presents.

"I can't," I said. "I've got band practice. I'll go to church with the guys."

My father took the news pretty calmly, although he kept nodding his head long after he should have stopped. It was my mother who got mad.

"That's ridiculous," she said. "Band practice on Christmas Eve. Who are you kidding?"

"Oh yeah," I said, "it's fine if a football team plays on Thanksgiving, but it's not okay if a band practices on Christmas Eve. Where's the logic in that?"

"Don't give me your logic. I just think you could put your family ahead of your friends for once."

My father touched her hand. "Forget it," he said. "I'm tired anyway. I'll go with you tomorrow."

I was hoping to make a quick getaway after supper, but my mother wasn't through with me. She waited until I was getting my coat out of the closet to play her final card.

"No sir," she said, positioning herself between me and the front door. "You're not going to church like that. You look like a ragpicker."

I was wearing school clothes, corduroys and a plaid shirt. I had changed into them specifically to avoid this argument.

"What do you mean?" I said. "You bought these clothes."

"You should wear a coat and tie to church. And no sneakers."

"Jesus never wore a tie," I said.

"What's wrong with you?" she asked. "Why do you hate me?"

"I don't hate you."

She made a big show of wiping her brow. "Whew. Thanks for the vote of confidence."

She turned to my father, who was sitting on the couch, ignoring us in favor of a crossword puzzle.

"Jim, tell Buddy he can't go to church like this."

He slapped the pencil against the paper in his lap and looked at us in total disgust. "Goddammit," he said.

In the end, we compromised. My mother went upstairs and packed my sportcoat, a white shirt, one of my father's ties, and my dress shoes in a shopping bag. I promised to change into the good clothes before going to church.

Ed's family was out visiting relatives, so Rockhead had the house to itself. Instead of jamming we raided the incredible collection of gift-box liquor under the tree. Ed's father drove a delivery truck for Budweiser, and all the liquor stores had given him bottles for the holiday.

Sally showed up a couple hours later, and we moved the party to her car. Cruising through town, I was struck by the darkness of the streets. When I was a kid, nearly every house was lit up and blinking this time of year. Ever since the energy crisis, though, people had been opting for solitary electric candles in their front windows. The whole world seemed to have outgrown Christmas along with me.

"Anybody see the *Grinch* the other night?" Sally asked. "That dog with the antlers is a real trip."

"Man, I hate Christmas shows," Ed said. "The fucking Grinch is bad enough, but the people are even worse. Perry fucking Como, Bing fucking Crosby, Donny fucking Osmond. Every washed-up moron in the universe gets a Christmas show."

"Bob fucking Hope," Dirk added.

"The King fucking Family."

"Andy fucking Williams."

"Just once," Ed said, "I'd like to turn on the TV and watch the Aerosmith Christmas special."

"Or the Dead," Sally suggested. "That would be cool."

"Not all those shows suck," I said. "Rudolph's pretty cool."

"Yeah, I like Rudolph," said Sally.

"Then you're both assholes," Ed told us. "*Rudolph the Red-Nosed Reindeer* is a totally fucked-up story."

"Gimme a break," Sally said.

"I'm serious," Ed said. "I've been thinking about it." He took a swig from his rum bottle, then a swig from the Coke can in his other hand. "I'm serious. First Santa cuts Rudolph from the reindeer team 'cause he's handicapped, he's got this electronic nose, right, and the next thing you know, everyone's down on Rudolph, his parents, his girlfriend, all the shithead reindeers. Am I right?"

"Yeah," I said. "So what?"

"So Rudolph runs away and hooks up with the misfits, who are completely excellent, but he has to leave their island because of the Abominable Snowman, right? So after putting Rudolph through all this crap, Santa has the gall to go back to him and beg him to guide the sleigh, because it's foggy out, and all of a sudden the electronic nose is this big bonus item. Now Buddy, if you're Rudolph, what do you do?"

"You're a reindeer," I said. "It's not like you have much choice."

"See," he said. "You're a chickenshit, just like Rudolph. But if it was up to me, I'd say, 'Suck my moosecock, Santa, I wouldn't guide your sleigh tonight for a million bucks, you fat shit.' "

After a while, Dirk broke the silence. "I was

just thinking," he said. "What if we changed our name to the Misfits?"

It was standing room only by the time Ed and I got to St. Elmo's. We had to squeeze in with the crowd of latecomers that had gathered in the rear of the church. At the altar, a choir of sixth-grade girls was singing "Silent Night."

I was feeling a little shaky. On top of the rum and coke, we'd smoked a joint before Dirk and Sally dropped us off, and now my head felt like it had been inflated to twice its normal size. A lot of adults were staring at me, their attention apparently focused on the shopping bag full of clothes that I'd set on the floor between my feet. To make matters worse, Ed snickered every time the choir hit a bum note.

Out of nowhere the organist struck a chord and a man in a dark suit shoved me backwards. It took a moment for me to comprehend that the man was an usher, making room for the priests and altar boys now entering the church to the tune of "O Come All Ye Faithful."

Our paperboy was at the head of the procession, carrying a tall silver crucifix. I winked at him, but his eyes remained wide and unblinking as he passed with slow, measured steps. I leaned forward to see if I could recognize anyone else. A priest swung a metal incense ball right in front of my nose. The smoke pouring out of it was heavy and

moist; one breath of it sickened me. A splash of
holy water got me in the face just as Monsignor
McGuire shuffled past with a ceramic baby Jesus
cradled in his arms. The doll was ugly—bald,
jowly, unhappy-looking—a miniature version of
the monsignor.

Mass started, and it was fun for a while to
watch the people sit, stand, speak, and cross themselves on cue. Every now and then, someone stood
up for no reason, glanced around in alarm, then
sat quickly back down. It was like a huge, easy-
going game of Simon Says.

Ed poked me. "Is that your dad with Toupee
Ray?"

My father was sitting on the right side of the
aisle. He was wearing his good blue raincoat, and
his hair was slicked back with Vitalis, curling a bit
above the collar. There was no mistaking the hair-
line next to his.

"Ray should have a raccoon tail hanging from
that thing," Ed whispered.

Bill Floyd was everywhere these days. Not
long ago I'd never seen him anywhere except
church. He came with his mother. Mrs. Floyd was
a blue-haired lady who wore a fur coat all year
round, except in summer, when she wore a stole
that came from the same animal. At the end of
mass, while everyone else filed out, she remained
on her knees. Her son sat beside her with his hands
in his lap, looking calm and unhurried.

I had a clear view down the narrow center aisle straight to the altar, where a priest I'd never seen before was going on in what may have been a foreign language, and I remembered that there used to be a bowling alley in the basement of the church. My father had worked there as a pinboy for a penny a game back in the days before automated bowling, the days of Latin Mass. Years ago, the basement had been renovated into a separate church, with indoor-outdoor carpeting and soft overhead lighting. They had guitar masses down there.

I started to feel a little sick. Had someone turned up the heat? I wanted to take off my coat, but the procedure struck me as impossibly complex, what with the noise of the zipper and all the elaborate arm movements, so I decided to leave it on and concentrate on remaining upright.

Monsignor McGuire was giving a sermon about the Immaculate Conception. "And the Wonder of Wonders, the absolute joyful mystery of our Savior's birth is that God saw fit that Mary remained without stain. Our Holy Mother was without stain."

Ed gave me an elbow. "What detergent did she use?" His voice was nearly as loud as the Monsignor's.

Heads swiveled from all directions to look at us. Out of the corner of my eye, I saw a hefty usher start toward us, and something about his sideburns made me sure he was an undercover cop. The last thing I needed was to get busted in church. I grabbed my shopping bag and pushed through the crowd into the vestibule. Without stopping to bless myself, I opened the heavy wooden door and stepped outside.

The fresh air only made me feel worse. It was too early to go home, and I couldn't think of any-place to hang out, so I had no choice but to try to walk off the nasty hum in my head. I wandered down Grand Avenue, past darkened shops and fac-tories, staring at my sneakers so I wouldn't have to look at the endless series of identical Santa Claus faces smiling down at me from the overhead wires. At Icee Freez, beneath the neon vanilla cone that had been turned off for winter, I stopped to take a rest. Someone had been using the parking lot to sell real Christmas trees. There were still a few left, scrawny spruces lying flat on the asphalt, cut down for nothing. Hoping to clear my head, I bent down over one to inhale the scent of the needles. It was a mistake. I puked on the tree, then re-mained on all fours until the spasms passed.

As soon as I felt a little better I dragged my shopping bag over to another, slightly larger tree. It occurred to me that I'd have to change into my good clothes if I wanted to avoid a scene at home. I unzipped my coat and draped it over the tree, as though covering a corpse. Then I took off my shirt. I pictured myself as one of those bare-chested drunks you see at football games, raising his beer cup to the TV camera while the fans around him shiver beneath layers of winter clothing.

It took me about six tries to get the tie right, and even then the skinny end was a little too long. I sat down on the tree trunk to put on my ridiculous shoes. They had three-inch plastic heels and were hopelessly out of style. Just last year, I had begged my parents to buy them for me.

When I walked through the front door, my mother was right where I knew she'd be—in the middle of the floor, wrapping a present. The Yule log was burning on TV.

"You're early," she said.

"We had to stand in the back. I left at the beginning of Communion."

"Oh." She measured a length of red ribbon and snipped it with her scissors.

I took off my coat and hung it in the hall closet. The coat slid off the hanger just as I closed the door.

"I saw Daddy with Bill Floyd," I said. "I guess he got a second wind."

"Why didn't you wait for a ride?"

"I don't know. I guess I felt like walking." My voice sounded as though a ventriloquist were standing behind me, pulling a string.

Her eyes narrowed. "You look funny. Are you all right?"

"I'm fine."

"Come here. Hold down this ribbon for me."

"Just a minute. I have to go to the bathroom."

"Come on. It'll only take a second."

I approached cautiously and knelt down. I placed my index finger on the ribbon and stared at my fingernail for what seemed like a long time, trying not to breathe in her direction. She never tied the knot. When I looked up, her eyes were sparkling.

"How could you?"

"What?"

"Don't," she said. "Don't make it worse. Just get out of my sight."

I woke up on top of my bed, feeling awful. My pants were off, but I was still wearing the shirt and tie I'd put on at Icee Freez. I forced myself to sit up. As soon as I loosened the tie, my head started pounding and I remembered why I was awake: I had to wrap the presents.

On my way to the bathroom for aspirin I stepped on something. I groped for the wall switch and saw, in the sudden nightmare brightness, that my mother had left scissors, tape, and wrapping paper outside my door.

The picture on front of the Pepperoni and Assorted Cheeses Gift Pack was almost enough to make me puke again, but somehow I managed to pull myself together. When I was finished I gathered the gifts in my arms. They looked like they'd been wrapped by a six-year-old.

Downstairs, Bill Floyd was stretched out on the recliner, fast asleep. He was flat on his back with his hands behind his head. Every few seconds a blinking light illuminated the room. The light came from a large, five-pointed star on top of the tree, a star I'd never seen before.

I set my presents under the tree. When I stood up the star blinked and I got a good look at Bill Floyd. He was snoring softly, and I felt a strong urge to shake him by the arm and wake him up. I wanted to watch him sit up and glance around in confusion, his toupee comically askew on his head, trying to figure out where he was.

I poked him once, but he only mumbled a vague protest. His face was peaceful, and it was suddenly strange to think of him waking up, putting on his coat, and trudging home through the darkness. The star blinked again. It was strange to think of him opening the door and stepping inside the big empty house that was waiting for him.

# You Start to
# Live

It was just my luck to get Coach Bielski for driver's ed. Even when I played football, he hadn't been that crazy about me. He didn't like my attitude, the way I'd shrug when he asked me why I'd thrown a bad pass or missed a tackle. And he didn't like the way my hair stuck out from the back of my helmet or sometimes curled out the earholes. He'd tug on it at practice and say, "Cut that fucking hair, Garfunkel, or I'll cut it for you. I just got a chainsaw for my birthday." (He always called me Garfunkel, because of my hair and because he'd once seen me in the hallway, strumming someone's guitar. To Bielski, Simon and Garfunkel represented the outer limits of hippiedom.)

He was late for our first meeting. It was January and cold in the gym, but Bielski was dressed, as usual, in tight blue shorts and a gray T-shirt, the uniform that had made him a legend among Harding High football fans. He wore it every year to the Thanksgiving Day game, even if there was snow on the ground or a temperature in the single digits. People loved to see him standing on the rock-hard field, breathing smoke, dressed like it was the middle of summer.

He stopped at the edge of the basketball court to watch some guys shooting hoops, then continued over to the bleachers, where I sat waiting for him in the second row, wearing my blue suede coat.

"Well, well," he said. "Looks like Art Garfunkel wants to drive."

"You start to live when you learn to drive," I said, quoting from a late-night TV commercial.

Bielski shook his head. "Do yourself a favor, Garfunkel. Lay off the wacky weed. It's not doing wonders for your IQ." He glanced at his clipboard. "Is Laura Daly here?"

I joined him in scanning the empty bleachers. "Doesn't look like it."

"Thanks for the input, Garfunkel."

He handed me the clipboard, then dove to the floor and started doing marine push-ups. He always did push-ups when there was time to kill, partly because he was a show-off, and partly because he was a genuine fanatic. He did a hundred without breaking rhythm—I counted the hand claps—and was breathing more or less normally when he stood up. I gave him back the clipboard.

"Do me a favor, Garfunkel. Go see if Daly's in the hallway."

I didn't have to go far. Laura and her boy-friend were right outside the gym door, making a spectacle of themselves. Keith was backed up against a locker, cupping Laura's ass with both hands. She was on tiptoes, wearing the white nurse's dress that was mandatory for girls in the Beauty Culture program, licking his ear with an odd thoroughness, like a mother cat cleaning one of her kittens. I watched them for a while, then went back in the gym.

"She's right outside," I said to Bielski.

"Did you tell her to get her butt in here?"

"Not really."

Bielski tapped my head a few times, like he was knocking on a door. "You know what your problem is, Garfunkel? You're a spectator. You're happy to just stand around and watch. You don't take charge of a situation."

He strode out to the hallway and blew three shrill blasts on his whistle. "Break it up," he shouted. "Or take it to the Holiday Inn. No sex in the hall."

Laura followed him inside. Her blond hair was messed, but she didn't seem the least bit embar-rassed. I noticed a couple of greasy fingerprints on her dress when she sat down. Keith's hands must have been dirty from auto shop.

Bielski stuck his finger in her face. "Listen

up," he said. "I don't care what you do on your own time, but this class is my time. When that bell rings, you're mine, understand?"

He started a speech about how seriously he took driver's ed, but was interrupted almost immediately when Tammi Phillips tapped him on the shoulder. Tammi was a cheerleader who spent a lot of time around the coaches' office. She was small and had a cute upturned nose. Everything about her was girlish except her breasts, which were huge, way too big for her body.

"Coach," she said. "Telephone."

"Thanks, sweetheart."

Without a word, Bielski turned and jogged across the gym to the coaches' office. Tammi walked back in the same direction. The guys in gym class stopped playing basketball and exchanged glances as she passed.

Laura and I sat together without speaking. After about ten minutes she stood and stretched; her dress moved way up her thighs. She caught me staring, but only raised her eyebrows when she finished yawning.

"I'm going," she said. "See you Thursday."

I stayed put until the end of the period. Bielski never showed up.

I had a hard time learning to drive. Bielski said I thought too much, and he was probably right. I hadn't expected to have to think at all and was startled by the complexity of driving, the need to calculate risks and make snap decisions while moving. I expected the car to make decisions for me, and when it didn't, I panicked.

"Change lanes," Bielski said.

In the mirror, I saw a van bearing down in the left lane; my hands tightened on the wheel. Should I accelerate and cut in front of it? Or should I slow down and let it pass? I had to think fast, but my mind was blank, humming like a refrigerator. I followed my gut instinct and slammed on the brakes in the middle of St. George Avenue. The tires squealed; Bielski and I snapped forward and back in our seatbelts.

"Sorry," I said.

His eyes were wide, frightened. Laura giggled in the back seat, and I spent the rest of the day running stop signs and missing turns. When we finally got back to school, Bielski took out a handkerchief and wiped his forehead.

"Land ho," he said.

Laura drove one-handed, like an old pro. She was such a natural that Bielski let her take us on the Parkway our third week out.

"Don't worry," he told her. "It's a piece of cake. Just get in your lane and stay there."

It was a sunny day, the first in weeks, and we were heading south. Traffic was light. Laura and Bielski were discussing a TV movie that I hadn't seen. From what I could gather, it was about a woman who suffers from amnesia after a car accident and falls in love with her doctor. Laura liked the movie, but Bielski thought it was unrealistic.

"Come on," he said. "If all you did was watch movies, you'd think amnesia was a common thing. It's ridiculous. When was the last time you met someone with amnesia?"

"I can't remember," Laura said, and they both laughed.

While they talked, I gazed out the window at the other drivers. I saw a woman screaming over her shoulder at her kids, who were pounding each other in the back seat, and a guy in a business suit singing into an invisible microphone. I saw a nun eating a McDonald's hamburger in a station wagon. There was even a man who was reading a book. He was holding it up with one hand and moving his eyes rapidly from the page to the road.

One day in February, Bielski didn't show up for class. Laura and I sat in the bleachers for about twenty minutes, watching the guys in fourth-period gym play their usual lethargic game of basketball while the jayvee wrestling coach, Mr. Guido, looked on in disgust. I nudged Laura.

"You wanna go smoke a joint?"

Her face perked up. "You got one?"

It was the early lunch period, so we didn't have to use any elaborate maneuvers to get outside. We just walked through the cafeteria and out the door. We crossed Fillmore to Seventeenth Street, a dead end where students parked when the school lot was full. We sat on the curb in a narrow space between two cars. There was a leafless hedge at our backs, a rundown house across the street.

We had trouble lighting the joint. It was a windy day and the matches kept going out. I crouched in front of her to block the wind. She had the joint in her mouth with both hands cupped around one end. Our heads were close together, and she smiled at me as I struck the match.

Until driver's ed, we hadn't known each other at all. We came from different towns—Harding was a regional school—and took different classes. I was College Prep; she was Beauty Culture and Distributive Education, which was another term for work-study. She got out of school an hour early every day to work at Marcel's Beauty Chateau. Mostly she swept hair off the floor and stuffed it into plastic bags. She said Marcel sold it to a wig factory.

"I'm freezing," she said. "It's a good thing I put these pants on."

In the past couple of weeks she'd taken to wearing jeans under her white dress. At first I thought it looked strange, but I was beginning to get used to it. She wore the same pair of Levi's every day. They had patches on the knees and "Laura + Keith 4 Ever" written in Magic Marker on both thighs.

"I'm cold, too." I shifted position so our knees were touching.

"Keith wants me to marry him," she said.

"Wow."

"I know. It's pretty intense."

"I can't imagine being married until I'm about thirty."

"Really?" she said. "I can't imagine being thirty."

"It's like driving," I said. "Remember when you thought you'd never be old enough to drive?"

"I've been driving since I was twelve," she said. "My dad taught me."

We sat quietly and concentrated on passing the joint.

"So what do you think?" she said.

"About what?"

"About me and Keith."

"I don't know. Do you love him?"

"Sometimes. We have really great sex."

I dropped the roach and watched it smolder. Then I stepped on it and smeared it across the pavement. She touched my hand. "I hope I didn't embarrass you."

I shook my head. Out of nowhere a tingling rush traveled up from my feet and branched out through my body. I looked at Laura and started to laugh.

"You know what?" she said. "You need a haircut."

"Thanks a lot."

"I didn't mean it like that. I just think you'd look really cute with short hair. Long hair's out."

"I don't know," I said. "I don't wanna look like a disco boy."

"I could do it for you. We give free haircuts on Friday mornings. You could come tomorrow."

"No way. I heard about those free haircuts. Didn't Phyllis Lavetti go bald from one of them?"

"That was a perm," she said. "You'd just be getting a trim." She put her hand on my knee. "You'd look really cute, Buddy. The girls wouldn't be able to resist you."

"They'd find a way."

The school bell rang, and I felt cheated. Laura put her arm around my shoulder and kissed me on the lips.

"Thanks for getting me stoned. It was fun."

I helped her up and we started back to school. My body felt bouncy and light, like I was walking on the moon. The driver's ed car drove by just as we reached the corner of Fillmore.

"Oh shit," Laura said. "We're busted."

But Bielski drove right by. He pretended not to see us. Tammi Phillips was sitting in the front seat, but she ducked down as soon as we saw her.

• • •

I woke up the next morning and looked in the mirror. My hair was flat on one side, frizzy on the other. Laura was right: I needed a trim. It was a kind of defeat, admitting that to myself, a surrender of principle. I hadn't volunteered for a haircut since seventh grade.

I got a pass out of second-period study hall and went upstairs to the Beauty Culture room. I had never been inside and was surprised to see how closely it resembled a real beauty parlor. There was a row of four barber chairs facing a mirrored wall, a row of overhead hairdryers, even a waiting area up front, with women's magazines scattered on a table. There was a pungent chemical smell in the air.

At the far end of the room, a group of girls— most of them wearing jeans under white dresses— stood in a semicircle and watched their instructor, Mrs. Frankel, take bobby pins out of her mouth and jab them into the muddy hair of a middle-aged woman who appeared to be fast asleep in the chair. Closer to me, a lady crossing guard sat beneath a humming dryer, smoking a cigarette and paging through a magazine. I hesitated in the doorway, intimidated by the sight of so many females in one room.

Mrs. Frankel noticed me first. She was a hefty woman in a pale green smock, with a black beehive hairdo and slashes of purple makeup on both cheeks.

"Come on in, honey," she called out. "We won't bite."

Laura rushed across the room. "I'm so glad you came. You're gonna get the works."

She began by washing my hair. I leaned back in a reclining chair, my neck resting comfortably in a grooved sink. She sprayed my hair with jets of warm water, then massaged apple-smelling shampoo into my scalp. Her hip pressed firmly into my shoulder.

"Does this feel good?" she asked.

I closed my eyes and smiled at the ceiling. After the rinse, she rubbed my head with a towel and led me to a barber chair in the main room. Before she started cutting, she spun the chair around so it faced away from the mirror. Instead of looking at myself, I was staring at the crossing guard, who glanced up from her magazine to give me a friendly smile.

It was the slowest haircut I ever got. Laura would make a tentative snip with her scissors, then step back to consider her next move. After a while, she settled into a steady, thoughtful pace. I didn't mind. All I was conscious of was her physical presence. Her fingers on my jaw. Her breasts against my arm. I had an erection the whole time.

"Damn," she said. "You have some weird cowlicks."

I didn't start to worry until the second time she said, "Oops." Twice after that she called some friends over for whispered conferences; once she crossed the room to talk to Mrs. Frankel. She was still cutting when the bell rang for third period.

A few minutes later she spun me around. I almost didn't recognize myself. My ears and nose looked immense, like I had borrowed them from one of my uncles, and my head seemed slightly off center—no matter how I held it, it seemed to tilt to the right. Laura stood behind me with her hands on my shoulders, trying gamely to smile.

"So," she said. "What do you think?"

"It's short," I said. There was a strange hollow feeling in my chest.

"Don't worry," she said. "You'll look great when it grows in."

When I walked into history class, the girls stared at me and the guys in the back of the room shrieked in mock horror. After class, I asked my friend Ed if I really looked that bad. He opened his locker and gave me his black winter cap, the kind burglars wear on television.

"Keep this for as long as you want," he said.

On Saturday morning my mother gave me a twenty-dollar bill and sent me to the Head Shed to see if Mario couldn't make me "look like a human being again." Mario got angry when I told him what happened.

"Beauty Culture," he said, shaking his head.

"Just because they have scissors doesn't mean they know how to cut hair."

"She was my friend," I said.

"Big deal," he said. "I got lots of friends. But when I had to get my appendix out, I went to see a doctor, *capice?*"

There was a party that night at Valerie McDonough's house. Valerie was the Harding Hawk mascot; she wore a bird suit and danced around the sidelines at football games. She also sold pot. Through these activities, she knew a wide variety of people.

It was a pretty good party—her parents were in Florida—but I wasn't in a very sociable mood. It happened to be Valentine's Day, a stupid holiday, and a miserable one if you're alone and have a bad haircut. On Friday, the *Harding Herald* had put out a special issue in which people wrote messages proclaiming their love or secret admiration. I read the whole thing, but my name wasn't mentioned.

I stood in a doorway near the keg and watched the girls dancing in the living room. Most of them looked thoughtful and repeated a few simple movements over and over, while others whirled across the floor, all flying hair and arms. For about the tenth time, someone came up behind me and yanked off my hat. Now that I was a little drunk, it didn't bother me so much. I didn't even turn around. A hand moved slowly through the stubble on the back of my head. Somehow, I knew it was Laura before I heard her voice.

"It doesn't look so bad," she said. "Who fixed it?"

"Some guy at the Head Shed."

"Are you mad at me?"

"No."

"Good." She slipped the hat back on my head and smoothed it over my ears. "I need to talk to you."

"Okay."

"I have my father's car. You want to take a ride?"

"Yeah. Just let me get my coat."

She followed me upstairs to the master bedroom. The coats were scattered on the bed, a tangled heap of them several layers high. Mine was the only blue suede coat in the bunch.

"Okay," I said. "Let's go."

She shook her head and pushed the door shut with her foot. She stepped forward and put her arms around my neck.

"Do you like me?"

I nodded.

"Do you really like me?"

I nodded again.

"I want you," she whispered.

It struck me as a corny thing to say, totally unlike her, and I almost laughed. But before I could, she put her tongue in my ear. My whole body shivered.

"Me too," I said, and we kissed, mashing our mouths so hard our teeth clacked together.

When we opened the door, Valerie was standing patiently in the hall with an armful of coats. She seemed surprised to see us but didn't say anything as she slipped past us into the bedroom.

Laura's father's car was a big old Impala with ice-cold seats and a bad muffler. We kissed some more while the engine warmed up, then cruised down North Avenue into Cranwood, past the strip of fast food places glowing bright and empty in the night. We drove past a theater just as the movie was letting out. Young couples streamed out of the door as if on a conveyor belt and scattered on the sidewalk.

"I'm sorry about your hair," she said. "I still think you're cute."

"Where are we going?"

"I'm not sure. You wanna go to my house?"

"I don't know. Do you?"

She bit her bottom lip and nodded.

"Okay," I said.

We turned off Orange Avenue into a section of Springdale known as the spaghetti streets. It felt like we were moving through a maze.

"Where's Keith?" I asked.

She shrugged. "Who cares?"

"Don't you?"

She shook her head. "Not anymore. We broke up tonight. He tried to give me a ring, but I wouldn't take it."

We pulled to a stop. Laura lived in a small house that was mostly hidden from the street by a big evergreen in the front yard.

"You'll have to be quiet," she said, fitting the key in the front door lock. "My dad sleeps on the couch."

"Your parents are home?"

"My dad is."

"Where's your mom?"

"Ohio, last I heard."

The door opened right onto the living room. Laura's father was sleeping on his back, breathing unevenly through his open mouth. One arm dangled off the couch. He stirred and mumbled something in his sleep. There was gunfire on TV, but I couldn't tell what show it was.

We tiptoed upstairs. Her room was small, the walls almost completely papered over with posters and photographs of Robert Plant and Jimmy Page. She lit a candle on the nightstand and turned off the light. The door locked from inside.

"Is this all right?" I asked. "What about your father?"

"Don't worry," she said. "He's out for the night. If he hears anything, he'll just think you're Keith."

We lay down on the bed and started rolling

around. After a while I started touching her through her clothes, but it only made her laugh.

"Look," she said. "Wouldn't this be easier if we got undressed?"

"Okay."

"You first," she said.

She sat on the edge of the bed and watched me strip.

"Those too," she said.

I stepped out of my underwear and was instantly embarrassed by my erection. There was something absurd about the way it called attention to itself, like an exclamation point or a funny hat.

"You're beautiful," she said, and I felt goosebumps rising on my arms and legs.

She pulled back the covers on the bed and I climbed in. The sheets were cold. She pulled her sweater over her head and reached back to unhook her bra. Her breasts were small, her skin ghostly pale in the candlelight.

"Here I am," she said, spinning slowly, like a model, wearing only socks.

I had spent so much time fantasizing about naked women that I expected the sight of one in real life to be a momentous event. But there was something strangely ordinary about the sight of Laura's body, her skinny arms and narrow hips, the tight, boyish curves of her butt.

"I knew this was going to happen," she told me. "Ever since the day we smoked that joint."

"Me too," I lied.

"It's mystical, Buddy. It was meant to be."

She got into bed and we found each other, her socks warm and scratchy against my cold feet. She kissed my chest and neck, then rolled me on top of her. Shivers passed through my body in taut, pulsing waves. She took me in her hand and spread her legs.

"Help me," she whispered, guiding me inside.

All I could do was gasp in astonishment. This is Laura, I told myself, my partner in driver's ed, but that daytime world no longer seemed possible as we slipped and writhed, locking together like parts of a single machine. Fucking. Screwing. The words popped into my mind, then dissolved instantly. Nothing had a name anymore.

A voice said, "Slower. Take it easy."

I opened my eyes. I opened my mouth.

A voice said, "Not yet," a second too late. My arms buckled and I collapsed on top of her, as startled as if I'd crashed through the ceiling.

"Shit," said the voice, and this time I recognized it as Laura's.

It took all the energy I had just to separate myself from her and flop onto my back. For a time, I felt like a stranger to myself. My body wasn't a body, but a humming void, peaceful and weightless. But the moment didn't last. The usual sensations returned to my arms and legs. The loud voice started up again in my head, the endless

151

drone of my own thinking.

Laura had rolled onto her stomach and buried her face in the pillow. When I asked if she was okay, all she did was shrug.

"I'm sorry," I told her. "I'll do better next time."

"It's okay," she said in a muffled voice. "There's nothing to worry about."

We got dressed and tiptoed back out to the car. With our clothes on, we seemed not to recognize one another. Except for directions about where to turn, we didn't say anything the whole way home. She drove faster than usual, like she was trying to get it over with.

After we kissed good night, I paused with one leg outside of the car. I wanted to tell her something that would do justice to the things I was feeling: that I thought she was beautiful, that I missed her already, that I would spend all night staring at the ceiling in my room, trying to remember the way she looked with her shirt off. But I chickened out.

"Well," I said. "See you in school."

She was absent on Monday and didn't answer the phone when I tried to call in the afternoon. By the time driver's ed rolled around on Tuesday morning, I was desperate to talk to her. I needed to know where we stood, what would happen next. I got to the gym a few minutes early, hoping we could have a few minutes alone, but Bielski was already there, doing jumping jacks by the bleachers. He was in high spirits when he finished.

"Garfunkel," he said. "Have a good weekend?" He held an imaginary joint to his lips and took a long toke. "Smoke a little dope?"

"Not me," I said, pulling off my hat. "I got a haircut."

He was impressed. "Jeez, Garfunkel. You look like a mental patient."

Laura was smiling when she entered the gym.

"You're late, Daly."

Bielski tossed the car keys to her, but she made no effort to catch them. She kept her hands in her coat pockets and watched them land at her feet on the hardwood floor.

"Elizabeth today," Bielski said. "Wolfgang's Sporting Goods on Broad Street. I need to pick something up for the indoor meet."

Laura and I lagged behind as we walked through the parking lot.

"Are you okay?" I asked.

"Yeah," she said. "Why?"

"You're not mad at me?"

She shook her head. "I'm not mad at anyone."

It was her turn to drive. She was quiet behind the wheel, and I wondered if Bielski noticed a difference in the car, if he sensed that things had changed.

"Guess what?" Laura said. We were stopped at a red light in Darwin.

"What?" Bielski and I blurted out, almost in unison.

"Do you guys notice anything different about me?"

She waited a few beats for an answer that didn't come.

"My hand," she said.

She twisted in the driver's seat and held up her left hand so Bielski and I could see the ring sparkling on her finger.

"It's a diamond," she said. "Keith and I are getting married this summer."

"I thought you two broke up." I was amazed at how normal my voice managed to sound, as though I were simply curious.

"We made up," she said. "We had a really long talk."

"Are you quitting school?" Bielski asked.

The light changed. "Not really. I'll get an equivalency degree at night. We've got it all figured out."

"How are you going to support yourselves?"

"Keith's a mechanic," she said. "I'm a hair-stylist."

Bielski shook his head. "You're too smart for that. You should go to college."

"What for?"

"What for?" Bielski said. "To get an education. Broaden your horizons."

"Oh yeah," Laura said. "And if I do really well, maybe I can be a gym teacher. Maybe they'll even let me teach driver's ed."

"You just better think about what you're doing," Bielski said. "Marriage isn't a date for the prom. If you make a mistake you'll have to live with it."

Laura's face turned red; her bottom lip trembled. She wiped her eyes with the back of her hand and glared at Bielski.

"And I was so happy," she said.

"Oh Christ," he said. "Garfunkel, why don't you take over."

I drove the rest of the way to Elizabeth. Traffic was heavy, but for the first time, I felt like I was part of it, like I had a rightful place on the road. I maintained a steady speed and changed lanes without hesitation. Bielski didn't seem to notice; he was busy examining a pink piece of paper he'd taken from his pocket, a receipt of some sort. I heard Laura sniffling in the back seat.

Bielski got out of the car at Wolfgang's and slammed the door. I watched through the plate glass window as he entered the store and shook hands with a stocky, gray-haired man wearing a suit and tie. The man disappeared down an aisle, and Bielski walked past a row of bicycles to a punching bag. He hit it twice, barely making a dent.

"You could at least look at me," Laura said.

"Why?"

"All right," she said. "Don't look at me. I don't care."

I was searching for something suitably nasty to say when Bielski came out of the store with his new discus. He was gripping it with one hand, like he just might send it flying into the middle of Broad Street. He looked pathetic, like he'd gotten lost on his way to the Olympics.

"Just so you know," Laura told me. "I'm three months pregnant."

That Thursday, Bielski let me drive on the highway. Laura cut class, so he was my only passenger. We took Central Avenue into Clark and followed the curving ramp onto Parkway South. It was a boring stretch of road, no scenery except bare trees, squat office buildings, and the pale gray sky.

On my way to homeroom that morning, I had turned a corner and seen Laura and Keith up against a locker, kissing and laughing. They hadn't even noticed me as I walked by. Only now, at sixty miles an hour, could I even think about it without wanting to punch a window. With my hands on the wheel, I felt better and stronger, no more alone than anyone else.

Memories of my time with Laura flashed by like billboards. Our faces in the mirror, looking scared. Her body in the candlelight. Her father mumbling in his sleep. *I want you.* When I remembered her saying that, I laughed out loud.

"What's so funny?" Bielski asked.

"Nothing."

"It's quiet without Daly," he said a moment later.

"I know," I said. "I miss her."

He nodded. "She reminds me of a girl I knew when I was your age. Arlene Muller. I still think about her sometimes."

I kept my eyes on the road and waited for him to finish the story. It took me a minute to understand that it was already finished.

# The Jane Pasco
# Fan Club

**I WAS** watching *Wake Up, America!* one gray
morning in 1978 when the show's host, Nancy
Vernon, almost made me choke on my Pop-Tart.

"You know," she said, in that soft, oddly intimate voice that made her such an agreeable
morning companion, "we hear a lot about the
habits and opinions of so-called Average Americans. But lately we've got to wondering: who are
these elusive creatures? Where do they live? What
are their hopes and fears?

"Well, *Wake up, America!* decided to find out.
After weeks of snooping and statistical analysis, our
staff located a town that can only be described as
uniquely ordinary. Darwin, New Jersey, isn't too
big and it isn't too small. The 5,342 people who
live there aren't rich and they aren't poor.
They're . . . well, they're just about average."

I was thinking I must have heard wrong—
Darwin, New Jersey!—when the video screen be-

hind her head blossomed with a face that didn't belong on TV. It was lumpy and mismatched, like a bad composite portrait, with beady eyes, a false-looking nose, and a high forehead decorated with thin strands of strategically combed hair. I felt a strange thrill. It was the first time I'd ever seen someone I knew on television.

"Mario Moretti is the mayor of Darwin. Good morning, Mr. Mayor."

The mayor straightened his tie and showed his teeth.

"Good morning to you, Nancy."

Nancy Vernon thoughtfully stroked her chin, as though she were about to address an important world leader.

"Tell us a little about your town, Mr. Mayor."

"Well, Nancy, there isn't that much to tell. It's your basic small town, a nice friendly place. Everyone knows everybody else."

He was at least right on that last count. Mayor Moretti, for example, had grown up with my father and coached me in the Little League. His wife had served with my mother in the PTA. His son Mike had gone out with my girlfriend for two years before breaking her heart. Now he wanted her back in a big way.

"What kind of problems does the town face?"

"We Darwinians are basically concerned with inflation, high taxes, drugs, crime, and the sky-rocketing cost of gasoline."

"Crime?" Nancy Vernon sounded a note of surprise. "Is there a lot of crime in Darwin?"

The mayor backpedaled. "Heck no, hardly any. Maybe a little shoplifting." His smile brightened. "If you want to get murdered in broad daylight, you can always catch the bus to Manhattan."

Nancy Vernon didn't crack a smile. "Mr. Mayor, we'd like to give our viewers a closer look at an Average American Town. Would you mind if we paid Darwin a visit?"

"We'd love to have you, Nancy."

"One more thing. While we're in town, we'd like to drop in on an Average American Family. Could you arrange that for us?"

"I'd be delighted."

The next day every family in town received a letter from the mayor's office inviting them to apply in writing to be featured on *Wake Up, America!* It said that although everyone was technically eligible for the honor, the show's producers had expressed a preference for a family of four, consisting of a blue-collar husband, a working wife, two kids (girl and boy), and a dog. Right after I read the letter I called my new girlfriend, Jane Pasco.

"Hey," I said. "It's too bad you don't have a dog. You could be on TV."

I meant it as a joke, but she didn't laugh.

"Jane?" I said. "Are you there?"

• • •

Mr. Pasco convinced Jane to go with him to the Humane Society. She dragged me along for moral support.

We passed through an anteroom filled with cats stacked one on top of the other in stainless steel cages. Most of them were fast asleep, despite the alarming volume of dog noise coming from the adjacent kennel. From a distance the barking had sounded relatively innocuous, but up close it took on an angry and desperate edge, as if each dog were crying out in its own private language:

"Take me!"

"Save me!"

"Hey you in the green shirt!"

"Help!"

The dogs were confined in two rows of remarkably clean cells separated by a cement walkway. The cells were narrow, about the size of bathroom stalls, with cinder block dividers and chain-link fencing across the front. Jane clutched my shirtsleeve. Her father adopted the cool, noncommittal air of a man browsing through a used car lot.

A Samoyed flipped her food bowl, sending dry kernels skittering across our path. A shepherd banged his head repeatedly against the fence. A handsome black Lab stood on his hind legs, barking spit into the air. A beagle frantically chased her tail.

"This is the one," Mr. Pasco declared.

He was pointing at a quiet, intelligent-looking mixed breed, identified by his information tag as "Sparky." He was a yellow dog with a dark face, flat ears, and sympathetic eyes. The tag said he was four years old and had been surrendered due to "owner allergy." He stared back at us and thumped his tail twice, as though he knew he'd been chosen. In spite of herself, Jane smiled.

Sparky was a good dog. When we took him for a walk that night, he moved at our pace without straining at his leash. At the park, he politely sniffed the other dogs, but showed no interest in fighting or humping.

"Well," I told Jane, as we followed Sparky down the dirt path, "even if you don't get on TV, at least you saved a life."

"I don't know," she said. "Dad's got his heart set on winning. He thinks it'll be good for Matt."

Jane's brother, Matt, had dropped out of college in the middle of his first semester. During a late-night acid trip, he had hallucinated that his dorm was on fire. He'd pulled the alarm, then braved the imaginary inferno to knock on doors up and down the hall, waking his neighbors and herding them to safety in their pajamas and robes. The administration had asked him to leave.

He came home and spent a couple of months in his room with the door shut, rereading *The Lord of the Rings* and cultivating a scraggly beard. Then, one bright morning in January, he hopped out of bed, showered, shaved, and put on his only suit. For the next day and a half, until the police made him stop, he went door-to-door, asking people to sign a petition in favor of making his birthday a national holiday: Matt Pasco Day.

On his rounds, he collected thirty-seven signatures, a bad reputation, and a girlfriend who was an even sadder case than he was. Pam Devlin had been a classmate of Jane's until junior year, when she suffered some kind of breakdown. First she stopped washing her hair; then her spine began to curve like an old lady's. She went for days at a time without speaking to anyone. Her parents blamed her friends for warping her mind. Her friends accused her parents of beating her for minor offenses, even of locking her in a closet once for trying to sneak out of the house in a halter top. She spent a year in some kind of institution, but looked no better on her return.

She and Matt became inseparable companions. Her parents, who had once been sticklers on such matters, no longer seemed to care if she spent the night—or several consecutive nights—away from home. By the time I started going out with Jane, Pam was pretty much a live-in guest at the Pascos'. Jane's parents weren't thrilled with the situation, but they accepted it. Pam was Matt's only friend. It was almost sweet to watch him guide her around the house, patiently explaining the operation of the toaster or the windowshades, as though she were an exchange student from another planet.

"It's funny to think of Matt on national TV," I said.

"I know." Jane shook her head at the thought. "Maybe he'll get in a plug for his holiday."

When we got back to the house, Mr. and Mrs. Pasco were standing on the front stoop, like a young couple posing for a picture. It was a heartwarming image until you got close enough to notice their expressions.

"Oh Janey," Mrs. Pasco began in a trembling voice. "We just got a phone call."

"It's Mike," her father explained. "He took an overdose."

Jane made a soft, strange noise; Sparky's ears stood up.

"Sleeping pills," Mr. Pasco continued. "He apparently meant business."

"But he's okay," Mrs. Pasco said quickly. "They had to pump his stomach."

We were at the bottom of the steps, they were at the top. I turned to comfort Jane, but she dropped Sparky's leash and rushed up the stairs, into her mother's arms.

For two years Jane and Mike Moretti had been one of Harding High's most conspicuous couples. He was a varsity soccer and baseball player, an all-around nice guy. She was a cheerleader and an excellent student, one of the cutest girls in school. They were always together. People claimed that they were secretly engaged.

It all changed one weekend of their senior (my junior) year. On Friday, Mike was holding hands with Jane. On Monday he had his arm around a hot sophomore named Sally Untermeyer, while Jane drifted alone through the halls, looking like she'd just donated several pints of blood. She told me later that the hardest thing about the breakup was cheerleading, having to smile like an idiot and pretend she was happy. Away games were especially painful since she had to ride on the same bus with Sally, who, as a member of the drill team, got to wear go-go boots and carry a disturbingly realistic wooden rifle.

Second semester, Jane and I were in the same American lit class. Late in February, Miss Maxwell assigned us to do a collaborative oral report on *The Great Gatsby*. Sitting close together in the library, talking in whispers, we debated the virtues of telling a story through the eyes of a minor character. At one point, Jane stopped talking and looked at me, and I had the feeling that she was seeing me for the first time.

"Have you ever had a broken heart?" she asked.

"Me?" I said.

She nodded.

"Yeah," I told her. Laura Daly's face flashed in my mind. Only a few weeks had passed since the night we'd made love. "I have one right now."

"I thought so." Jane sat back and smiled. "We should go to the movies sometime."

My ears started ringing when she said that. I was thrilled by the idea, but also frightened. I didn't see how I could possibly live up to her standards. Mike was tall, athletic, and already eighteen years old. He drove a red Firebird. I was only sixteen, five-foot-five, and recovering from a bad haircut. I didn't have a driver's license, let alone a hot car.

But none of that seemed to matter to Jane. She picked me up in a station wagon on Friday night and laughed at everything I said. After the movie she took a detour through Echo Lake Park, pulling into this deserted parking area. She had her arms around me before I could even undo my seatbelt.

"God," she said, as I gasped for breath in the wonderful interlude between our first and second kiss, "it's nice to be with someone normal for a change."

"Normal?" I mumbled, disappointed by the word.

"Mmm," she said, sliding her hand underneath my shirt and up my stomach. Her fingertips traced lazy spirals on my chest. "I'm tired of crazy people."

I closed my eyes and surrendered to her definition. "You're in luck," I told her. "I'm as normal as they come."

As soon as Jane and I went public as a couple, Mike had a change of heart. He broke up with Sally and started pestering Jane, calling her every night, leaving presents by her locker, and generally making a spectacle of his misery. It turned her into a nervous wreck.

"Look," I said, "do you still have a thing for him?"

She shook her head.

"Then why don't you tell him to buzz off?"

"You don't understand, Buddy. He's not as strong as he looks. He gets really depressed."

"That's not our problem," I said.

But it was. Mike followed us around. I caught glimpses of him in the mall and at the bowling alley. I turned around one night in the Cranwood Theater and saw him sitting three rows back with this queasy expression on his face. A few days later, he was standing by my locker when I got to school.

"What do you want?" I asked.

Tentatively, as though he thought I might be electrified, he reached out and laid his hand on my shoulder.

"Isn't she terrific?" he said. "Don't you love the way she smells?"

"Come on, Mike. Don't be a creep."

He winced and withdrew his hand. "We should be friends, Buddy."

"Why?"

Smiling mysteriously, he pulled a white business card out of his shirt pocket and handed it to me. My name was typed in capital letters across the front of the card.

"Congratulations," he said. "You're an official member of the Jane Pasco Fan Club."

He still had this comical grin on his face, like the whole thing was a big joke. I shook his outstretched hand.

Jane drove me home from a party the following weekend. We kissed for a long time before I got out of the car. Then I shuffled backwards up the front walk, waving to her taillights. When I turned to go up the steps, I almost tripped over Mike.

"What'd you do tonight?" he asked cheerfully.

"Go home," I said.

"What was she wearing?"

"Please go home."

He didn't answer right away. When he did, I could barely hear him.

"Can I come in with you?" he asked. "I'm not feeling too well."

I hesitated. I wanted to help him, but didn't know how to do it without complicating things even further. Above all, I didn't want to encourage him.

"Sorry," I said.

I squeezed past him and went inside. I don't know how much time he spent on the porch that night, or what kinds of thoughts went through his head as he watched the streetlights shine on the empty pavement. I do know that five days later he made a serious attempt at suicide.

Jane visited Mike in the hospital on Sunday afternoon. I called her in the evening for an update.

"He's okay," she said. "We watched a golf tournament on TV."

"Why'd he do it?"

"He didn't say."

I let the silence thicken and dissolve before changing the subject.

"Can I come over tonight? Maybe we can take Sparky for a walk or something."

"Buddy," she said, "we have to talk."

"About what?"

"I need some time off. I can't be anyone's girlfriend for a while."

"How long's a while?"

"I don't know. Just till things get back to normal." Her voice had been calm and flat throughout the conversation, but now it cracked. "God,

Buddy, he tried to kill himself."

Jane didn't deserve any more trouble. She'd already been through a rotten year. In September, the factory where her father worked had shut down without warning. He spent a few months looking for work, then got depressed and settled in for the long haul on the living room couch. He scratched off a minimum of five Instant Lottery tickets a day and sometimes threw tantrums when he lost, claiming that everybody won big money but him.

After twenty years as a housewife, Mrs. Pasco had to get a job to help pay the bills. All she could find was slave-wage secretarial labor for a tyrannical insurance agent who used Grecian Formula, drove a red Corvette, and liked to remind her that she could stand to lose a few pounds. She had trouble getting up to speed and routinely stayed in the office until seven at night to finish her typing.

When I started going out with Jane, she was rushing home from cheerleading practice to cook dinner for her father, Matt, and Pam, and then spending another hour cleaning up, so her mother wouldn't burst into tears when she walked through the door into a messy house.

Then, late in March, the family hit a run of good luck. Mrs. Pasco switched to a better-paying job at a bigger company, where she had a humane supervisor and a realistic workload. Mr. Pasco did some under-the-table interior painting for a friend and found himself unexpectedly swamped with offers from the friend's neighbors. He began dreaming of a father-and-son business, and convinced Matt to help him out for a few hours a day. Even Pam Devlin seemed to be improving. She took better care of herself and started pitching in with the housework. Sometimes she even laughed at Mr. Pasco's corny jokes.

April was a wonderful month. Jane invited me to her senior prom and decided to teach me how to dance. Whenever we had time we went down to her basement rec room, put on a stack of old 45s, and worked on my rusty moves.

The night before Mike took his overdose, we had an impromptu dance party with Matt and Pam. Matt danced like an acidhead, planting his feet and waving his arms, octopuslike, overhead. Pam marched triumphantly around the room, pumping her knees and elbows like a majorette. Mr. and Mrs. Pasco came downstairs to tell us to lower the volume, but somehow ended up teaching us all how to jitterbug.

On Monday, I restricted myself to smiling at Jane in the halls and transmitting telepathic love messages across the room in English class. It was fun in a childish sort of way, like a staredown or a breath-holding contest, but it got old fast.

I stationed myself in front of her locker on Tuesday morning. She wasn't happy to see me.

"What now?" she groaned, as though I'd done nothing but bother her since she woke up.

"I just wanted to see how you were."

"Terrible. If you really want to know."

"You want to talk about it?"

"The only thing I want is to graduate from this fucking school, leave town, and never come back."

I was surprised by the bitterness in her voice. Seniors talked like that all the time, but Jane sounded like she meant it.

"Never come back?" I said. "But then you wouldn't get to see me."

She gave me a cold, level stare.

"I'd get over it."

"I guess you would."

Her expression softened a little.

"Don't hate me," she said.

"I couldn't. Even if I wanted to."

"Don't be too sure."

On my way out of school that day, I saw her climb into a pistachio-colored Cadillac with a forest-green roof. It was the mayor's car, and the mayor sat stiffly in the driver's seat, wearing state trooper sunglasses and a red polo shirt. For a moment, even though I knew they were going to the hospital, I felt an involuntary pang of jealousy. And then I just felt miserable.

For two seasons, Mike and I had been teammates on Moretti Motors, a Little League team sponsored and managed by his father. I played shortstop; Mike played first. He followed me in the batting order and led the team in home runs. Whenever we won, he would shake up his soda can for a long time before popping the top. Only a few years had passed since our days in the Little League. But that afternoon, as I watched the Cadillac vanish around a corner, it already felt like a lifetime.

Jane's absence on Wednesday came as a relief. In the preceding days, it had begun to seem like she, Mike, and I were cut off from the rest of the world, floating like astronauts in a private capsule of sadness. But now the spell was broken and I found myself miraculously returned to earth, to a high school full of friendly people with simple lives. My natural optimism revived itself. I realized that Jane would eventually return too—though it might take her a lot more time—and that when she did, I would be waiting for her. Our dancing lessons would resume.

After school I went to work in the deli. Even the meat case seemed comforting in its familiarity, the cold cuts arranged in perfect order on their white metal trays. Around four o'clock Mrs. Trunchka came in, right on time. She was one of our regulars. Every day she bought a pound of spiced ham.

"I just got a call from my sister-in-law," she

said, as I moved the cool slab of meat back and forth across the whirring blade. "She looked out the window about an hour ago and who do you think she saw across the street?"

"Who?" I caught the limp slices as they fell and slapped them on the scale.

"Nancy Vernon. From *Wake Up, America!*"

"Oh yeah," I said. "I forgot about that."

"Well," said Mrs. Trunchka, "she gets out of a limousine and walks right up to Marge Pasco's front door, like they're old friends or something. My sister-in-law almost had a coronary."

Carefully, I dropped the last slice on the pile and switched off the machine.

"The Pascos?" I said, trying to keep my voice within normal range. "They're the Average American Family?"

Mrs. Trunchka nodded. "That's right," she said. "With that crazy son of theirs and everything. But you know how it is." She held up two crossed fingers. "They're like this with the mayor."

"Is she still there?"

"Probably. She was ten minutes ago."

After Mrs. Trunchka left, the store was quiet. I held onto the cool marble counter and tried to think. I decided not to wake Mr. Freund from his afternoon nap and explain the situation. Even though it could have cost me my job, I just hung the "Closed" sign in the front door and took off full tilt down Center Street, still wearing my tat-

tered white apron, which was stained with mustard, beef blood, soup, and coffee.

The cops had closed Maple Street to traffic. A
red, white, and blue *Wake Up, America!* van and a
white limousine were parked in front of Jane's
next-door neighbor's house. Across the street a
crowd of about thirty people had gathered behind
a line of yellow police barricades: neighborhood
kids straddling bikes, young mothers with bored,
thumb-sucking toddlers, nosy retired men, and a
couple of celebrity creeps, including one guy in
an army jacket clutching a back issue of *TV Guide*
with Nancy Vernon's picture on the cover.

I pushed my way to the front of the barricade,
wedging myself between Pam Devlin and the guy
in the army jacket. Pam looked so good I almost
didn't recognize her. Her hair was freshly washed,
and she was wearing lipstick and a pretty blue
sailor dress that belonged to Jane. She gave me a
quick dazed smile when I touched her shoulder,
but immediately turned her attention back to the
Pascos' front door. Mayor Moretti stood next to
her in an expensive gray suit, nervously tugging
on his earlobe. The breeze had messed up his hair,
blowing the long strands off his bald spot back to
their point of origin. I wanted to tell him how
sorry I was about Mike, but realized that this
wasn't the time or place for sympathy.

Maple Street was a nondescript block of nearly
identical split levels, each with a driveway, a patch

of lawn, and a bay window. Grass and trees didn't thrive there, so the street usually looked bleak compared with the rest of Darwin. But that day, just in time for the cameras, spring had arrived. Technicolor azaleas and forsythia had exploded into bloom. The scrawny curbside tree trunks disappeared into clouds of pale green blossoms. Even the corner Stop sign seemed unusually red. Jane's beige house looked different, too. An unfamiliar flower box full of tulips jutted out from beneath the bay window; a brand new backboard and rim had sprouted over the garage door. A supernaturally orange basketball lay motionless in a driveway black with a fresh coat of sealer.

The crowd began to clap as two crew members—one with a camera, the other with a clipboard—scurried down the front steps and positioned themselves on the lawn, facing the door. Nancy Vernon emerged first, looking statuesque in a crisp navy suit that contrasted well with her stiff yellow hairdo. The stoop gradually filled up with the entire cast of family members: Mrs. Pasco in an apron, Matt and Mr. Pasco in paint-splattered work clothes, Sparky in a red-bandana collar, Jane in her cheerleading outfit, Mike Moretti in a suit and tie.

The world, which seconds before had seemed clear and bright, turned suddenly murky, as though I were watching it on a set with bad reception. But what I saw was real: Mike was standing behind Jane, with both hands resting on her shoulders. He was so tall that their heads appeared to be stacked one on top of the other, like a partially completed totem pole. They were both smiling.

The mayor's face was transformed by the sight of his son. He stuck two fingers in his mouth and whistled. "Mikey!" he yelled in a booming voice I remembered from Little League. "Way to go, Mikey kid!"

At the same time, the guy in the army jacket started jumping up and down, waving his *TV Guide*. "Nancy!" he shouted. "I love you, babe."

I felt like screaming too. I had this crazy idea that if I yelled her name just right—the way Dustin Hoffman yelled "Elaine!" at the end of *The Graduate*—Jane would come bounding down the steps into my arms. Millions of Americans would witness our defiant embrace. But when I opened my mouth, all that came out was a loud moan, an animal whimper of defeat.

Pam turned and looked at me. She was sucking on her index finger, her eyes big and glassy. The next thing I knew she was in my arms, sobbing fiercely against my shoulder, while Nancy Vernon and the Average American Family stood together on the porch, waving to the nation.

Several years later, Mike Moretti and I played on different teams in the Darwin summer softball league. After a game one night, still in our grass-stained uniforms, we ended up sitting together at the bar in Jimmy B's Lounge, buying each other drinks. Things were going well for both of us. I would soon begin my senior year in college. He had just graduated from Rutgers and was about to enter law school at the University of Texas. He looked healthy and said he'd developed an interest in politics.

There was a strange intensity to the meeting, as if we'd once been best friends. The drunker I got, the closer I felt to him. Late in the night, he flipped open his wallet to a photograph of a pretty, round-faced girl with dark hair.

"This is Maggie," he said proudly. "I think she's the one."

"Great," I said, patting him on the back. "She's really cute."

"What about you?" he asked. "You with anyone?"

I didn't have a picture of my current girlfriend, but something compelled me to open my wallet and fish out the wrinkled white card he'd given me in high school certifying my membership in the Jane Pasco Fan Club.

"I don't know why," I told him, "I still carry it around."

Mike stared at the card for a few seconds, then shook his head. The juke box cast an eerie red glow across his face.

"That was a strange time," he said. "Do you see her anymore?"

"Not for years."

I did see Matt and Mr. Pasco on occasion. They had a thriving home improvement business—John Pasco & Son—and did a lot of work around Darwin. I also saw Pam Devlin from time to time. Sometimes she recognized me, usually not. She'd gone off the deep end since Matt broke up with her, and now spent her days wandering around town in dirty clothes, talking to an imaginary companion.

The Pascos' segment on *Wake Up, America!* had lasted only a couple of minutes. It analyzed their grocery bill in minute detail and portrayed them as "American Dreamers in an era of belt tightening." It could have been about anyone. But Jane never recovered from the experience. She remained moody and distant in the months that followed, and wouldn't answer my calls. As soon as she got the chance, she left town for college and, as far as I knew, never came back.

# Just the Way
# We Were

Dave Horvath and I went to Towne & Country Tuxedo to get ourselves outfitted for the senior prom. On his girlfriend's instructions, Dave chose a powder blue tuxedo to match his eyes. I selected a tan tux with lighter beige piping on the cuffs and lapels. The cummerbund, bow tie, and pointy shoes came in a color called eggshell.

Dave was an unlikely candidate for the passion that had claimed him. He was scrawny and good at math, with a pale hangdog face and an expression generally frozen somewhere between shock and sadness. Until one fateful night in the winter of our senior year, he'd never even had a girlfriend. Then he walked into McDonald's, saw Anita draining the golden oil from a basket of fries, and fell in love on the spot. "I looked at her," he told me, "and I just knew." She must have known too, because she agreed to ride with him to Echo Lake when her shift was done. He claimed she unzipped her ugly brown uniform that first night. He said she tasted like burgers.

On our way home from Towne & Country, Dave told me to check the glove compartment if I wanted to see something cool. What I found, hidden beneath the road maps and travel packets of Kleenex, was a pair of yellow cotton panties, limp and slightly frayed at the edges. There was a tiny smear of dried blood in the crotch.

"They're Anita's," he said.

"She let you keep them?"

"She's got a really open mind about stuff like that."

I put the panties back in the glove compartment.

"What about Sharon?" he asked. "What's she like?"

He was looking for a swap, a secret for a secret, and I would have been more than happy to comply. But I'd never come close to seeing Sharon's underwear, let alone keeping some as a souvenir.

"She's different," I said.

Dave's laugh was short and explosive.

"I bet she is."

Sharon had moved to Springdale in November of our senior year. She just appeared out of nowhere in four of my classes, this skinny, birdlike girl with watchful eyes and frizzy brown hair that seemed to have been scribbled on her head by a cartoonist.

She wasn't that pretty, but I couldn't stop staring at her. I had this weird feeling she was going to be important.

We had the same lunch period. She ate by herself, then wrote in a spiral notebook until the bell rang. I pulled a chair up one day and introduced myself. She nodded politely, but her pen kept moving across the page.

"Hey," I said, "you writing a book?"

She ignored me, encircling the notebook with her left arm, as if to prevent me from copying. The tip of her tongue protruded slightly, giving her an air of deep concentration.

"This might sound strange," I said, "but the moment I saw you I knew we were going to be friends."

She gave up and closed the notebook.

"Who are you? The Amazing Kreskin?"

"Come on," I said. "It's just a feeling. Haven't you ever had a feeling about someone before?"

"Yeah," she said. "But not about you."

I was persistent. She was lonely. Within three weeks we were eating together every day. I found out that she came from Richards Grove, a wealthy town about a half hour away, and that her parents were divorced. She talked a lot about San Diego, where her father lived with his new wife (as part of the custody arrangement, she and her sister spent summers there). Sharon wasn't crazy about her father, but she loved California: the people had open minds, and the ocean turned purple at sunset.

My friends assumed from the start that I was putting the moves on her, but they were wrong. We didn't even see each other out of school until January, when she invited me to her sister's tenth birthday party.

"My mom's worried," she said. "She's afraid I don't have any friends."

"Oh, so now I'm the token friend."

She patted me on my hand. "I hope it's not too much trouble."

They lived in an apartment complex near the highway. Sharon's mother answered the door. She tugged on her hair and pretended to scream when I mistakenly called her Mrs. Phelps.

"Please," she said. "Call me Delia. I'm not Mrs. Phelps anymore, thank the Lord."

Delia's face was an older version of Sharon's—sadder, slightly bloated. The skin below her eyes was loose, darkened like a bruise. Her clothes, though, reminded me of a high school girl: tight designer jeans, red high heels, fuzzy cowl neck sweater.

"Don't mind me," she said. "Tonight's my dancing lesson. My boyfriend and I do Arthur Murray. It's a blast."

"Sounds great."

"Careful," Sharon called from the kitchen. "She'll try to teach you the Hustle."

Everything in the apartment radiated a uniform, vaguely depressing newness—the furniture, the carpet, the appliances, the paint on the walls. Gail, the birthday girl, sat hugging her knees in front of the TV, studying a rerun of *The Brady Bunch*. With her pudgy face and sandy hair, she could have been a Brady girl herself.

"Are you Sharon's boyfriend?" she asked.

"No," I said. "We're just friends."

On TV, Mr. Brady lectured his boys on tolerance of the opposite sex. Girls are different from us, he said. We have to learn to respect and love them for who they are, as difficult as that might be. In another room, Mrs. Brady told the girls the same thing about boys. Sharon lit the candles on the cake.

Gail sulked through our spirited, nearly melodic rendition of "Happy Birthday," but she blew out the candles with a vengeance. Delia asked her if she made a wish.

She nodded. "I wish we could go move back to the old house."

Delia winced. "Now, honey . . ."

"The move's been tough," Sharon told me.

We started in on the cake. No one seemed to know what to say.

"So why did you move?" I asked. It was something Sharon had never really explained. "I hear Richards Grove is a pretty nice place."

They stopped chewing and looked at me. Sharon said it wasn't that nice. Delia said they needed a change. Gail glowered at her plate.

"Great cake," I said.

After Delia left, I hung around for a couple of hours with Sharon and Gail, playing a card game called Uno. In the months that followed, I became a kind of permanent guest at the apartment, spending three, sometimes four evenings a week there, doing my homework, watching TV, helping Sharon babysit Gail. I was never quite sure if I'd adopted them or if they'd adopted me.

My parents assumed Sharon was my girlfriend and kept agitating for a meeting. When I tried to set them straight, they just smiled and told me to invite her over anyway. I finally gave in, just to get them off my back.

I warned Sharon not to expect too much. My parents were nothing like Delia. They weren't particularly talkative, didn't go to Arthur Murray or hold surprising opinions. They spent most nights in front of the TV, complaining that nothing was on.

Despite my concerns, it turned out to be a pleasant evening. We played Scrabble, then sat around the table for a couple of hours, eating Oreos and listening to my parents trade sob stories about their deprived childhoods. Around eleven-thirty, way past his bedtime, my father bounded upstairs and returned with his air force photo album.

"I spent two years in the Far East," he informed Sharon. "It was the adventure of my life."

"That's right," my mother added. "The Philippines still haven't recovered."

I'd seen the album several times, but that night it seemed unfamiliar, full of new information. Sharon pointed to a picture of my father standing near the wing of a propeller-driven airplane.

"You were handsome," she told him. "You look just like Buddy."

My father and I blushed simultaneously. It was the first time she'd complimented my looks.

My mother laughed. "That was a good thirty pounds ago."

"I was twenty then," said my father. "Not much older than Buddy is now."

A sleepy-looking guy with dark wavy hair appeared frequently in the album, making faces or holding devil's horns over my father's head.

"That's Billy Penny," he said. "My best friend. We met in Basic and stuck together the whole way."

"Where's he now?" I asked.

"Dead." My father cleaned cookie crumbs off the table, lifting them with a moistened fingertip. "Car accident. We'd only been stateside for a week. We were planning to drive to California, look for work out there."

It was funny to hear my father talk about a best friend. He certainly didn't have one now.

"That's terrible," said Sharon.

My father scratched his head. "Life's a funny thing. If Billy hadn't died, I might never have met Ann. Buddy might not have been born."

All three of them stared at me, as if to verify my existence. I didn't like the idea that someone else's death was indirectly responsible for my life.

"Hey," I said. "Don't look at me."

Gail and Delia were asleep when we got back to the apartment. I followed Sharon into the dark kitchen. She asked if I wanted a soda. I asked if I could kiss her.

She leaned against the refrigerator and hung her head. "Oh boy," I heard her whisper. She didn't resist when I pressed my lips against hers, but she didn't exactly respond either.

"Did you enjoy that?" she asked. The question wasn't angry or flirtatious.

I said I would have liked it better if I thought *she* liked it. She sighed and ran both hands through her wonderful hair.

"Okay," she said. "Let's try again."

The second time didn't work either.

"I'm sorry, Buddy. I don't think this is a good idea."

"Why not? Don't you like me?"

"I got involved with a friend once before. It was a complete disaster."

"We're different," I said.

She chose that moment to open the refrigerator door and take out a bottle of Pepsi.

"Please," she said. The bottle made a kissing noise as she twisted the cap. "Let's just forget this happened."

Sharon just wanted things to stay the way they were. She said she thought of me more as a brother than a boyfriend. I did my best to act like a brother for a couple of weeks, but it got tiring. I had to change tactics.

I tried to hurt her into loving me back. I started showing up late at the apartment, leaving early. I talked a lot about other girls I found attractive.

"I'm not standing in your way," she told me. "If you want to go out with someone, be my guest."

It was already April, a good time for a senior fling. With time running out, people made themselves available. It was possible to experiment, to compromise, to make up for lost opportunities. I left a party one night with Janice Maloney, a sweet, chubby girl I'd known since kindergarten. She wasn't that drunk, but she let me touch her anywhere I wanted. Then she held me tightly and wept.

"I'm going to miss you," she said. "I'm going to miss everybody. I just wish this year would last forever."

• • •

Every time I said the word *prom* around Sharon, she laughed and stuck her finger in her mouth. I understood her reaction, but I also happened to be suffering from a severe case of premature nostalgia. Now that I was about to leave Harding, I was haunted by all the experiences I'd missed. I felt like I'd spent too much time on the sidelines, at the edges of high school. But the prom, that was dead center. I decided to go without her.

I made a mental list of candidates but couldn't work up the nerve to ask any of them. One by one, my possibles found other dates. With only three days to go before the deadline, I finally managed to ask Patty Green, this cute junior, my partner in phys ed archery. She blushed and told me I was a week late: she'd already agreed to be a mercy date for her brother's best friend Bruce Davis, a nice guy with a heartbreaking case of acne.

Comforted by the knowledge that I'd at least made an effort, I resigned myself to staying home. I made plans with a group of guys who were holding a "Fuck the Prom" party. Then, miraculously, the day before the deadline, Sharon popped the question. It came out of the blue, at the tail end of another sad night.

"You're kidding," I said.

She shook her head.

"*You* want to go to the prom?"

"It's my mom," she whispered. "She's afraid

I'll regret it for the rest of my life if I miss the stupid thing."

In a funny way, her answer came as a relief. I thought at first that she was just feeling sorry for me and was offering herself as an act of mercy. At least this way she could believe that I was doing her a favor. And I, in turn, could wear my rented tuxedo with a shred of dignity.

The dress she wore belonged to her mother. It was a strapless pink chiffon with a flaring knee-length skirt, a party dress from the fifties. Her shoes were black, her anklets lacy white. With her hair pulled back in barrettes and pink lipstick that echoed the dress, she looked like a beautiful dream of herself.

Elegantly, as though she did it every day, Sharon held out her bare arm so I could slip the wristlet of flowers over her hand. It was a slow and somber operation. When it was done, she pinned a flawless white carnation to my lapel, and her mother began to weep.

"Mom," said Sharon. "Please."

"I can't help it," she said. "You just look so perfect together."

"Welcome Prom Couples!" said the marquee outside the Blue Spruce Manor.

The Manor had a plain exterior—white stucco washed with blue and red lights—but inside it was Glitz City. A shimmering teardrop chandelier dripped from the ceiling; the wallpaper felt like velvet. In the corner, camouflaged by tall fake plants, a medieval suit of armor stood guard over a miniature waterfall that gushed mysteriously from an opening in the wall. Sharon's eyes widened.

"Wow," she said. "Is this tacky or what?"

I gave her an affectionate poke in the ribs. "Loosen up. It's your senior prom."

"Oh yeah." She reached up and straightened my bow tie. "I almost forgot."

Flashbulbs popped as we entered the banquet hall. I was struck by an unexpected wave of emotion at the sight of so many familiar, radiant faces: these were the people I'd grown up with, the ones I'd soon be leaving. The band was playing "We May Never Pass This Way Again," and my vision went a little blurry. Sharon on my arm, I nodded and smiled like a movie star on Oscar night as we threaded our way to Table Eight. Our tablemates had already arrived. Except for Dave Horvath, I wasn't really friends with any of them.

Dave and Anita both had lipstick on their faces. Anita surprised me: she was short and thick, with a pug nose and a loud laugh, not a person I'd see making French fries and fall in love with. But Dave kept touching her every few seconds—gropingly, the way a blind man might—as if to reassure himself that she was real, and not some glorious mirage.

Dave's friend Ted Wenkus had also brought a girl I'd never seen before, a tomboy with a Prince Valiant haircut and a crooked smile, the kind of girl who was probably good at pinball and could blow interesting smoke rings. Ted reminded me of a giraffe: he had a freakishly long neck topped by a head the size of a cantaloupe. I knew him mainly by reputation. Over the winter he'd figured out how to get an outside line from the chem lab phone, and had amused himself by calling faraway places and asking about the weather. It became a strange in-joke for a couple of weeks. People would grab you in the hall and say, "It's snowing like crazy in Billings, Montana. Pass it on." Ted and his date were both pretty drunk.

Rita Sue Branzino, on the other hand, looked like she could have used a drink. A talented tap dancer and a shoo-in for valedictorian, Rita Sue was headed for Princeton in the fall. Every Halloween she dressed up like a different piece of fruit, and she always won first prize for best costume. Her boyfriend was tall and blond, surprisingly handsome, though he seemed nearly radioactive in his dazzling white tails.

"This is Robert," she said, smiling stiffly. "He's going to Harvard."

Ted Wenkus and his date howled with laughter.

"This is Suzy," Ted announced. "She's going to the bathroom."

• • •

Somehow I'd gotten it all wrong. Even though I knew we had to share a table with three other couples, I had allowed myself to imagine the prom as an intimate, romantic scene, a last chance for Sharon to fall in love with me. Instead we had to listen to Rita Sue enumerate the wonders of Princeton while the band (Jimmy Dee and the Dee-Lites) cranked out a bouncy Carpenters' medley, and Dave and Anita French-kissed between mouthfuls of bloody prime rib.

The drinking at the previous year's prom had apparently gotten out of hand, prompting our advisers to announce a hard-line anti-alcohol policy. If you wanted to drink (like everyone at Table Eight with the exception of Rita Sue), you had to hide in a bathroom stall to do it. As the night progressed, we spent more and more time in the downstairs rest rooms, boys with boys, girls with girls. Our secret party required fancy flask relays and elaborate comings and goings, lending the evening an aura of teamwork and intrigue.

I'd never seen Sharon tipsy before. She seemed more animated than usual, a little less vigilant. When Suzy asked for a dance partner, Sharon was the first volunteer. She was a cool and limber dancer, sexier than I expected.

"Sharon's great," Dave told me as we made our fourth trip to the rest room.

"Thanks," I said.

We pressed ourselves against the bannister to make way for Vince Fowler, Harding's superstar heavyweight wrestler. Vince had chosen to wear his bow tie on his forehead, making his face look like a frightening birthday present.

"Fuckin' prom!" he shouted, slapping us five as he passed.

The rest room attendant greeted us with a nod. His job, as far as I could see, entailed sitting on a stool and listening to the Mets game on a transistor radio.

I followed Dave into an empty stall. He flipped down the toilet seat and climbed on top of it, so anyone passing would only notice one pair of shoes. He took a long swig of blackberry brandy and handed me the flask.

"We're all going to the Arrowhead after this," he said. "You guys should come."

"What's the Arrowhead?"

"You don't know?"

I shook my head.

"It's a motel on Route 9. Twenty bucks a night, no questions asked."

Someone knocked on the door. Dave dropped into a squatting position. The latch rattled.

"Open up. It's only us."

Giggling, Ted and Robert piled into the closet-size stall. Without a word, they joined Dave on top of the toilet, all three of them balancing precariously on the horseshoe-shaped seat. The flask made another circuit. Ted nudged Robert. They were drunker than we were and had become fast friends.

"Dude," he said, "you've got to tell these guys."

"Huh?" Robert seemed a little bewildered. He had one hand on Ted's shoulder and was marching in place on the seat, lifting one white shoe, then the other.

"You know," Ted told him. "Puke City."

Robert moaned. "Man, that was a secret."

Ted turned first to Dave, then to me. He had a big smile on his little face.

"Every time they have sex, Rita loses her lunch."

Dave and I exchanged grimaces.

"During?" I asked.

"After," said Robert. "She can't help it. It's some kind of reflex."

Dave reached past me and patted Robert on the arm.

"That must be awful."

Robert nodded. "It kind of detracts from the experience."

"Well," said Ted, "just hope they have barf bags at the Arrowhead."

When I got upstairs, Rita Sue was alone at the table. Sharon, Suzy, and Anita were on the crowded dance floor, where a forest of waving arms spelled out the chorus of "YMCA."

"Hey," I said. "How come you're not out there?"

She shrugged, took a sip of water, and smiled. "You and Sharon make a good couple."

"Robert's a nice guy."

"I'm glad you're all getting along," she told me. "He can be a little shy."

Daria Peck was elected Prom Queen. When Mr. Landon announced her name, she let loose with a bone-chilling wail, as if she'd just been informed that her whole family had gone down in a plane crash. She shrieked again when Mrs. Petrosky crowned her with a silver tiara and the crowd burst into applause.

The lights in the banquet hall grew dim.

"Ladies and gentlemen," said Jimmy Dee, "I'd like to invite each and every one of you onto the dance floor for the final and most special song of the evening, the one that you, the Harding High Class of '79, have chosen as your prom theme. And while you hold on tight to that certain someone, why not take a moment to reflect on the meaning of this wise and beautiful song of love, composed by the multitalented Mr. Billy Joel."

Despite my write-in vote for Aerosmith's "Dream On," the class had chosen "Just the Way You Are" by a wide margin. I took Sharon's hand and led her onto the dance floor as the music began. Jimmy Dee's electric piano was sick with reverb, his voice soggy with emotion as he begged his lover not to change the color of her hair.

"I hate this song," Sharon whispered.

Beams of light ricocheted off the spinning disco ball, painting the dancers with swirling stripes of color. The floor was so packed, all you could do was hold your partner and sway a little from side to side. Couples around us began making out; it reminded me of that scene in *Carrie*, just before the blood started to fly. I glanced hopefully at Sharon. She smiled back. But before I could kiss her she pulled me close, resting her forehead on my collarbone.

I brushed my fingertips across her shoulders, inhaling the peculiar and luxurious atmosphere of her hair. She didn't protest, so I stroked her neck, ran my knuckles over the ridges of her spine, traced with my palm the soft slope where her hips began. Her body was warm and my hands trembled. I wanted that stupid song to last forever.

I was nervous when we got into the car. We still hadn't figured out what to do next.

"They're all going to a motel," I said.

"I know. Anita asked if we wanted to go."

"Should we?"

She stared straight ahead through the windshield, clutching her white shawl tightly to her throat.

"What would we do at a motel?"

"Would it be so awful?"

"I guess we could watch TV," she conceded.

"That last dance," I said. "Did you feel my hands?"

"They were shaking."

"It was nice to touch you."

"I had a good time," she said. "It was fun being part of a group like that."

The cars around us pulled out, forming a long line at the exit. We were like a small island of indecision in a dark corner of the parking lot.

"What should we do?" I asked.

She gave a little shrug and gazed down at her lap. The barrettes were gone; her hair hung mop-like, concealing her face. She tried to tuck some behind her ear, but it spilled back out. She lifted her head and fixed me with a suspicious look.

"Can I trust you?"

"Sure."

"I'm going to tell you something. But first you have to promise to be nice to me."

I promised. She unclasped her evening bag and took out her wallet. She removed a photo-graph from a laminated pouch and pressed it into my hand.

"Remember," she said. "You promised to be nice."

I flipped on the dome light and found myself looking at a school portrait of a girl with olive skin and straight dark hair. She wore a white turtleneck and a dreamy yearbook expression. Her nose was big, but it seemed to fit with the rest of her face.

"That's Lorraine. She was my best friend."

"So?"

"We got into big trouble."

"What kind of trouble?"

She bit her lip. "You have to understand. We spent a lot of time together."

A middle-aged waitress with a platinum bouffant stepped out the front door of the Manor. She lit a cigarette and exhaled into the night. The smoke hung momentarily in the air, a ghostly, quivering blob. I turned off the light. Sharon took back her picture.

"Her brother found her diary," she said. "It had some stuff about us."

"Stuff?"

"Her parents freaked out. They made her transfer to Catholic school. They wouldn't even let us talk on the phone." She snapped her fingers. "It happened like that."

"Wait up," I said. "What did she write in the diary?"

"I don't know. I didn't see it."

My hands were shaking again.

"Did you guys do something?"

"It happened," she said. "I don't see why everybody has to flip out."

"How many times?"

"I don't know. What difference does it make?"

I had a bad moment. The interior of the car seemed to expand, until a vast distance separated me and Sharon on the front seat. Pictures from dirty magazines flashed through my mind. I turned away from her and found myself startled by the sight of my own tuxedo, the eggshell cummerbund bulging like a pot belly. A sickly laugh escaped from my throat.

"What's wrong?" she asked.

"What's wrong?" My voice was loud with indignation; I didn't want it to sound like that. "What's wrong? You invite me to the goddam prom and then—"

She cut me off. "Look, I'm sorry I brought it up. I thought you would understand."

"I'm not sure I do."

"Fine," she said. "Maybe you should just take me home."

"Maybe I should."

The key was in the ignition, but my hands remained frozen in my lap. We just sat there like people at a drive-in, watching the waitress finish her cigarette. She dropped it on the pavement, stepped on it, and went inside.

"Why do you think we moved here?" she asked.

"Because of that?"

She waited for me to look at her, then nodded.

"You're kidding."

"I thought it would blow over, but it kept getting worse. Kids started saying stuff to Gail, and my mother just couldn't deal with it anymore."

"God."

"You think we deserved that?"

I shook my head, remembering the way she'd looked her first few days at Harding, so anxious and alert, the way she had hugged her books to her chest, and how badly I'd wanted to get to know her. I remembered, too, how she had always changed the subject when I asked about her old school and the friends she'd left behind.

"I wanted to tell you a few times," she said. "But I lost my nerve."

"You ever hear from her?"

"I write her letters, but I don't send them." She smiled. "I have this dumb fantasy she'll come visit me in college, and I'll dump this stack of like a hundred letters in her lap, and she'll read them and know everything that's happened to me."

I could see it. Two girls in a bare room, envelopes everywhere.

"Don't forget tonight," I told her.

Sharon looked at me. Her face was a question, close enough to kiss.

• • •

The front office of the Arrowhead Motel was constructed to resemble a gigantic roadside tepee. The desk clerk, though, was an Indian from India. I expected him to give us a hard time about our age and prom clothes, but he completed the entire transaction without making eye contact or saying anything except the price of the room. I signed us in on the register as "Mr. and Mrs. Billy Joel."

The room was small, decorated in dark brown and burnt orange. It smelled of an ongoing conflict between mildew and Lysol. A picture of the Eiffel Tower hung crookedly over the bed. Through the thin wall, we could hear the couple in the next room having sex. The man's name was Jack.

"Well," said Sharon, "at least it's no one we know."

The black and white TV had no vertical hold. No matter how many knobs I twisted, the picture just kept rolling by, like a broken slot machine.

"Oh no," said Sharon. "We're stuck in the Arrowhead with no TV. This is one version of hell."

I made a quick trip to the yellow, slightly funky bathroom, and returned just in time to hear the action in the next room come to a surprisingly abrupt halt. Sharon was standing by the bed, examining a green metal box on the night table. It had a coin slot but no instructions.

"What the heck," she said.

She took a quarter from her purse and

dropped it in. To our amazement, the bed began to rumble and vibrate. We dove on for the ride, rolling toward the center of the saggy mattress. We felt only a gentle trembling at first, but it grew gradually stronger, and then stronger still, until it seemed, for a few turbulent seconds, that it wasn't just the bed, but the earth itself that was shaking beneath us. When it was over, we stared at each other in stunned silence.

We giggled all the way through the second quake. By the end of the third, we were laughing so hard that Jack from next door started pounding on the wall. Lucky for him, we were all out of quarters.

# Wild Kingdom

**M**r. Norman died the summer after my first year in college. I had insomnia that night. I was lying in bed thinking bad thoughts about my ex-girlfriend and her new boyfriend when my bedroom walls started pulsing with pink light. I got up and went to the window. The ambulance was right next door.

My parents were already on the front porch when I got there, my mother wide awake in her robe, my father yawning in shorty pajamas. We watched silently as the first aid squad carried Mr. Norman out of his house on a stretcher. Mrs. Norman came out right behind him in the company of a fat policeman. She wore a windbreaker over a long filmy nightgown that swirled delicately around her legs as she walked. The cop led her down the driveway and past the ambulance to a patrol car parked across the street. He opened the passenger door and helped her inside, almost as though they were going on a date. Both vehicles sped off without sirens.

We didn't find out Mr. Norman was dead until the following evening, when his wife called and asked if I would be one of the pallbearers at his funeral. Her request surprised me. Mr. Norman and I had been on neighborly terms, but we were too far apart in age to ever really be friends. When we saw each other, we said hello.

"I'd be glad to," I said. "He was a good man."

I expected my parents to be upset with me for saying yes, but Mr. Norman's death seemed to have wiped his slate clean with them. My father shook my hand. "It's a good thing you're doing," he said.

The wake was at Woodley's Funeral Home. My parents and I were numbers 7, 8, and 9 on the Register of Mourners, but when we entered the viewing room, the only people there were Mrs. Norman, her daughter Judy Klinghof, and a clean-cut guy I assumed was Judy's husband. Mrs. Norman was holding a handkerchief to her mouth and sobbing. It sounded like she had the hiccups.

Mr. Norman was laid out in a half-open coffin that seemed to be floating on a bed of flowers. My parents knelt at the padded altar in front of him and bowed their heads to pray. I glanced over my shoulder at Judy Klinghof, whom I hadn't seen for years. She had changed from a beautiful hippie girl into this plain-looking woman with rose-tinted glasses and a perm. She was whispering something to her husband, who for some reason had taken off one of his shoes and was holding it up to the light.

When my parents were done, I got down on my knees and made the sign of the cross. Mr. Norman wore a blue pinstriped suit with a tiny American flag pinned to the lapel. He reminded me of an astronaut strapped into a capsule, calmly waiting for liftoff.

I was nine years old the first time I saw him. For my family, at least, it had been an ordinary fall Sunday. After church, we drove to Jersey City so my mother could visit her mother in the nursing home. We made the same drive every week. On the way, we passed a garbage dump that had been on fire for more than twenty years. My father told me that every time the firemen put out the blaze, it started up again a few hours later, so they finally decided to just let it burn. Some days the smoke was so heavy it was like driving through fog; other days you would just see a bonfire or two, as though people were camping out on that mountain of trash, maybe roasting marshmallows. A few miles up the road, we passed a sprawling junkyard where crushed car bodies of every imaginable color were stacked six and seven high.

Only my mother went into the nursing home. My father and I stayed in the station wagon and tuned into the Giants game on the car radio. The Giants were awful, but it was easy to imagine otherwise, listening to Marty Glickman's play-by-play crackling from the dashboard. "Ron Johnson takes the handoff fakes right spins left breaks a tackle and struggles forward before being buried beneath a wave of red jerseys for a gain of . . . one yard."

A while later, my mother returned carrying a grocery bag filled with Grandma's dirty laundry. She passed the bag to me, and I stowed it in the back, holding my breath to avoid the smells. We got home in time to watch the Giants lose and then remained in front of the TV for the West Coast game at four o'clock. We ate dinner during the second half. Every time the announcer raised his voice, my father and I put down our forks and rushed into the living room to see the replay.

After the game, that lousy Sunday night feeling sank in. I had homework but couldn't tear myself away from the TV. While my mother worked at the kitchen table, writing checks and licking envelopes, my father and I watched Mutual of Omaha's *Wild Kingdom*.

I was closest to the hallway, so when the doorbell rang, I got up to answer it. I was barely on my feet when it rang a second time.

"Hold your horses," my father called out from the couch.

I flipped on the porch lights and pulled aside the curtain on the front-door window. For one strange moment, I thought I was watching an out-door television: right in front of me, on my own porch, a man was choking a woman, shaking her by the neck as though she were a rag doll. I let go of the curtain and walked backwards into the hall-way.

"Who's there?" My father was squatting inches above the cushions on the couch, not sure if he should stand up or sit down.

"It's for you," I said.

Just then the doorbell rang several times in rapid succession, making a sound like a pinball machine hitting the jackpot.

My father rushed outside. "Hey! HEY!" I heard him shout. "Not on my porch!" He stuck his head inside the door. "Honey! Call the po-lice!"

When my mother hung up, I stepped onto the porch to let my father know the cops were com-ing. He was standing between the man and the woman, holding them apart like a boxing referee. "Just calm down," he was saying. "Just everybody calm down."

The strangler was a big guy, but not scary-looking, not the type you'd expect to find mur-dering a woman on your front porch. In fact, he looked like he was about to cry. He punched him-self in the leg and said, "I had a good life. I was happy. And that . . . that *whore* next door ruined it. It's all her fault."

He pointed to the small gray house where Mrs. Klinghof lived.

"You bastard," the woman said. "Don't blame her." Her words came in gasps, as though she'd been running windsprints.

"Hey!" my father broke in. "Watch your tongues. Both of you." Then, softly: "Go on inside, Buddy."

I stood in a daze in the middle of the living room. On TV, the white-haired guy from *Wild Kingdom* had changed out of his safari clothes. He was dressed in a suit, sitting on a stool in an otherwise empty room. "As Jim found out tonight," he said, "the African jungle is a dangerous place. But you don't have to be standing in the path of a charging rhinoceros to put yourself and your family at risk . . ."

Outside, there were sirens.

On the way home from school a few days later, I saw the strangler in front of Mrs. Klinghof's house. He was unloading suitcases from the trunk of a car.

"You must be Buddy," he said, stepping onto the sidewalk to block my path. "I'm Mr. Norman. We're going to be neighbors." He stuck out his hand. "Come on. Shake."

We shook. For some reason, I wasn't scared. His hand was big and soft. "Nice grip," he said. "You're a pretty strong kid." He touched a green and red plaid suitcase with the tip of his workboot.

"Say, how would you like to carry this up to the porch for me? I'll pay you a quarter." He reached into his pants pocket, pulled out a handful of change, and gave me three nickels and a dime. The suitcase wasn't even heavy.

At home, my mother did her best to answer my questions. Her explanation was complicated but logical, like the solution to a word problem. Mr. Norman had been cheating on Mrs. Norman with Mrs. Klinghof. Somehow Mrs. Norman had found out, so now Mr. Norman had to move in with Mrs. Klinghof. Pretty soon, Mrs. Klinghof would become Mrs. Norman.

"Mrs. Klinghof has been very lonely since Mr. Klinghof passed away. Now she won't be so lonely anymore."

"But what about the other one?" I asked. "The lady on the porch?"

"She's better off too," my mother said, after a brief hesitation.

The late Mr. Klinghof had been my friend. We used to play catch on summer evenings, standing on our respective lawns, lobbing the ball back and forth over his driveway. He wore a tattered four-fingered mitt that looked like it belonged in the Hall of Fame. We were both Yankee fans, and he talked endlessly about the team, comparing current stars to the heroes of the past. Mr. Klinghof was personally acquainted with Phil Rizzuto, the great Yankee shortstop and announcer. Just before he died, he got me the Scooter's autograph, scrawled on the blank side of a panel torn from a Parliament cigarette pack. "Holy Cow, Buddy!" it said. "Best Wishes from Phil Rizzuto."

For a long time after his death, Mrs. Klinghof moped around the house, trying to keep herself busy with yard work. She raked the lawn even after all the leaves were gone, and swept the sidewalk once a day with a push broom. In the summer, she cut the grass with hand clippers instead of a mower. She was alone in the house. Judy had been living for years in a commune in Canada with her boyfriend, who was dodging the draft. My mother told me she hadn't even come home for her father's funeral.

Mr. Norman tried hard to be a good neighbor. He knew he'd made a bad first impression. He was always ready with a wave and an optimistic statement about the weather. He shoveled our sidewalk after snowstorms and gave my father helpful hints on lawn care, but it didn't work: my parents were barely polite with the Normans. They never stopped by the fence just to chat, the way they did with our other next-door neighbors.

The funeral was on Friday morning. I had the day off from the sheet-metal yard where I was working that summer, driving a forklift for minimum wage. My alarm clock didn't go off until eight, two hours later than usual. I had stayed awake thinking about Patty until almost three in the morning, so I was grateful for the extra sleep.

Patty was my ex-girlfriend. She was a year younger than me, a senior at Harding High. For most of my freshman year in college, we'd managed to conduct a fairly successful long-distance relationship. And then I botched it.

Near the end of spring semester, this girl named Brenda from my intro psych class invited me to a party in her dorm room. We slept together that same night. The next day I wrote a long letter to Patty, who was still a virgin. I didn't mention anything about Brenda. I just said that we should start seeing other people. Three days later Patty called. She was crying.

"I don't want to see other people," she said. "I want to see you."

Brenda and I only lasted a few weeks, just long enough to discover that except for the ability to get on each other's nerves, we had absolutely nothing in common. When I called Patty to apologize and patch things up, she told me she'd already started seeing Brian Kersitis, this guy in her class. I liked Brian; he was the lead singer in a pretty good heavy metal band called Warlock.

"I guess I messed up this time," I said.

"Yup," she said. "I guess you did."

I didn't realize how badly I'd messed up until I got home from college and didn't have anything to do at night. I had no desire to hang around the house with my parents, and I didn't feel like going to the woods to get wasted with my high school friends. I just wanted to be with Patty. I missed her even more now that it was graduation week. I should have been going to parties with her every night, drinking beer, sharing the fun. Instead I spent hours in bed with my eyes wide open, imagining her and Brian Kersitis in the back seat of a car. On the night Mr. Norman died, a dark brown Chevrolet zoomed by me while I was walking down Grand Avenue near McDonald's. The car was decorated with blue and gold streamers, the colors of Harding High, and the word "PARTY!" was soaped across the side in big letters. Patty and a couple of her friends were leaning out the windows, shaking their fists and screaming at the top of their lungs, the way you do when you graduate.

My parents had already left for work, so I had the house to myself when I got out of bed. After I took a shower, got dressed, and ate a bowl of cereal, there was still time to kill. I turned on the TV and watched a rerun of *The Munsters*, an episode in which Herman makes a fool of himself trying to win Eddie's love, only to find out that Eddie loved him all along.

At nine o'clock sharp, Judy's husband Bob knocked on the front door. He and Judy were staying next door, looking after Mrs. Norman. Since we were both pallbearers, Bob had suggested that we drive together to the funeral. Woodley's was providing limo service for Judy and Mrs. Norman.

Bob stepped into the hallway and shook my hand. He was a tall, baby-faced man with hair that was parted in the middle and feathered back over his ears. Like me, he was wearing a dark blue suit, but his tie was wide and colorfully striped, a bit too cheerful for the occasion.

"I'll be ready in a minute," I said.

"No rush," he said. "You got any coffee? There's only Sanka next door."

"I could make some. But doesn't the final viewing start in fifteen minutes?"

"I don't know about you," he said, "but I could do without the final viewing. I sat in the funeral home for two hours last night and two hours on Wednesday. That's enough for me."

Bob followed me into the kitchen. He sat down and drummed his fingers on the table.

"You ever been to a wax museum?" he asked.

I poured water into the coffee maker and tried to remember if I had. "I'm not sure. Maybe a long time ago."

"Judy and I were in Niagara Falls a few months back and we went to one. This was on the Canadian side."

"Yeah? How was it?"

"Awful," he said. "No one looked like they were supposed to. Bob Hope looked more like

Nixon than Nixon did. It was a rip-off."

"Sounds like it."

"Yeah," he said. "I'd forgotten all about it until I saw Jerry in that coffin. He looked like one of those wax statues. Some celebrity you never heard of."

I sat down while the coffee brewed. It wasn't a very hot day, but Bob's face was red and sweaty. There was a napkin holder on the table beside a bowl of artificial fruit. He took a peach-colored napkin and wiped the sweat from his forehead. "Christ," he said. "It's a scorcher. What a day for a funeral."

"How's Mrs. Norman holding up?"

He picked a plastic pear from the fruit bowl and examined it closely. He tapped it against the table a couple of times, then put it back. "Not too good. I think Judy's gonna have to stick around here for a few days to make sure she doesn't fall apart. I have to drive back tonight. Can't miss work tomorrow."

"Tomorrow's Saturday."

"I manage a restaurant," he said. "Saturday's our big day." He turned his head to check on the coffee. The pot was filling slowly, one brown drop at a time. He wiped his face with another napkin. "Christ, you wouldn't believe what it's like over there. Millie doesn't eat, she doesn't sleep, she just prowls around the house searching for God knows what. Like last night, three in the morning, she comes into our room, turns on the light, and shoves this can of shaving cream into my face. 'Here, Bob, I want you to have this. I bought it for Jerry, but he doesn't need it anymore.' " Bob shook his head. "This whole thing gives me the creeps. I mean it would be different if I knew him."

"You didn't know him?"

"We only met once. Last year at my wedding." Bob smiled at the memory. "Jerry was crocked. You should have seen him on the dance floor."

When I was a sophomore in high school, I spent most nights alone in my room learning to play the guitar. After a few hours of staring at my fingers, I'd put down the guitar and go for long walks around town to clear my head.

I used to meet Mr. Norman a lot on the quiet residential streets in our neighborhood. He walked slowly, with his hands jammed into his pockets, whistling melodies I recognized from the "beautiful music" station my parents listened to in the car. At first we just nodded and went our separate ways, but we bumped into each other so often that year that it became something of a private joke between us.

One night in late spring, he stopped at a corner and waited for me. It was earlier than usual, and he asked me if I wanted to watch the Yankee game at his place. His wife was bowling, he said, and he could use the company. I was glad for the chance to prove that I didn't share my parents' grudge against him.

It was strange to turn the corner and walk past my own house into his, as though I were another person. The house seemed not to have changed since the last time I was there, back when Mr. Klinghof was alive. It was still dark and cluttered, with the same peculiar smell in the air, a permanent odor of breakfast. There was even a picture of Mr. Klinghof on the TV set. He looked older than I remembered him, and had a sad, kindly expression on his face. I realized suddenly that I'd missed him.

Mr. Norman turned on the Yankees. I pretended to watch the game and waited for him to start a conversation. A couple of innings passed.

"You want something to drink?" he asked.

"Water would be great."

He pointed to the kitchen. "Glasses are above the toaster."

I turned on the faucet and let the water run for a while. The sink was filled with dirty dishes. I looked in the freezer for ice, but the old metal trays were empty, coated with frost.

Back in the living room, Mr. Norman said, "Millie tells me you're a big baseball fan." He had an unlit cigarette in his mouth that bobbed up and down as he spoke.

I took a sip of water. "I used to be."

He patted his thighs and chest with both hands, then spotted his lighter on the coffee table. "You got a girlfriend?"

"Not really."

He lit the cigarette and blew a long stream of smoke at the TV screen. He nodded thoughtfully, then reached under the couch and pulled out a thick stack of magazines.

I was used to seeing *Playboy* and *Penthouse*, but these magazines were different. They had names like *Swank* and *Juggs* and *Twat*, and the models in them weren't all young and beautiful. Many were older, tired-looking women who didn't appear to be enjoying themselves.

I was staring at a picture of a woman painstakingly shaving her pubic hair when Mr. Norman got up from the couch and came over to where I was sitting. He put his hand on my shoulder and leaned forward to get a better look, his face so close to mine that I could smell his hair tonic.

"Look at that," he said, shaking his head and rubbing his chin like a philosopher. "Amazing. Where'd she get those tits?"

We heard a car pull into the driveway. "Better give me those," he said. "She wouldn't appreciate me showing them to you." He shoved the magazines under the couch and quickly took his seat. He crossed his legs and looked perfectly relaxed by the time the front door opened.

Mrs. Norman set her bowling bag on the floor and smiled when she saw me. She was wearing lime green stretch pants and a double-knit top with big orange flowers on it. I noticed that she had a decent body for a woman her age.

"Buddy," she said. "How nice to see you."

"Hi, Mrs. Norman." I felt my face turn red. I remembered that years ago, on our front porch, Mr. Norman had called her a whore. At the time, I hadn't even known what the word meant.

"I better get going," I said.

"Don't leave on account of me." There was an odd singsong quality in her voice, and I had the feeling that she was flirting with me.

"It's not that," I said. "I have some home-work."

She pouted momentarily, but then her face brightened. "Okay, but before you go, just let me get my camera. I want a picture of this."

She left the room. I looked at Mr. Norman, hoping for an explanation, but he just shrugged. "Millie's camera-crazy," he said.

Mrs. Norman took two pictures of me and Mr. Norman sitting together on the couch. She used a flash, and when I got home, black spots were swimming in front of my eyes.

On the way to the funeral home, Bob asked me if I'd ever been a pallbearer before.

"Not me," I said. "You?"

"You probably won't believe this," he said, "but until two nights ago, I never even saw a dead body."

"Never?"

He ignored the question and started fiddling with some controls on the dashboard. "Could you roll up your window? I'm turning on the AC. It's like an oven in here."

The air conditioning came on full blast. I had to adjust the vent to keep it from gusting in my face.

"It's a weird thing," Bob said. "My father died when I was a little kid, but I didn't go to the wake or the funeral. Ever since then, whenever somebody died, I've always been out of town. Away at school, on vacation, whatever." He groped in his inside jacket pocket and pulled out a peach-colored napkin. He'd grabbed a whole stack of them as we left my house. He wiped his face, then crumpled the napkin and tossed it over his shoulder into the back seat. "I'm telling you, I wasn't ready for it. It shocked the hell out of me to see Jerry in that coffin. I just didn't expect him to look so goddam dead. Christ, it really gets you thinking, doesn't it?"

It was a beautiful day, and the streets of downtown Cranwood were bustling with people going about their business. I watched them through the car as they put change in parking meters and checked both ways before crossing the street, and they seemed familiar and alien at the same time, like sea creatures when you visit an aquarium. I thought about Mrs. Kelly, my sixth-grade math teacher, who died of a heart attack before she had a chance to give us our grades for the final marking period. On the night of her wake, a big group of sixth, seventh, and eighth graders met in the schoolyard and walked together to the funeral home to pay our last respects. No one expected us. Adults looked on in astonishment as we filed past the coffin, a seemingly endless line of girls in pretty dresses and boys in suits that didn't quite fit. Many of us were crying, even though Mrs. Kelly had been an unpopular teacher, known for giving pop quizzes and making kids stick gum on their noses if they were caught chewing it in class. I kept my composure until I reached the foot of the coffin; then I froze. I had never seen a dead person before and didn't know what to do next. There was a painful little smile frozen on Mrs. Kelly's face, like she was trying hard to be polite. The girl in front of me, Mary Jane Zaleski, leaned over and kissed her on the cheek, so when my turn came I did the same thing. I kept my eyes closed, and her face against my lips felt as cool and smooth as a blackboard.

"You're in college, right?"

Bob's question brought me back to reality. We were driving down a wide, tree-lined street not far from the funeral home.

"Yeah. I'll be a sophomore in September."

"You like it?"

"Beats working."

He nodded. "No kidding. I wish I was back in school."

The funeral home was a red brick house with a wide front door and a perfectly manicured lawn. Bob pulled into the circular driveway and found a parking space behind the building, next to the dumpster. He left the engine running and turned to me.

"Appreciate it while you can, Buddy. These are the best years of your life."

"If they are, I'm in big trouble."

He sat there for a few seconds, gripping the steering wheel with both hands, gazing straight ahead at a sign that read, "FUNERAL PA-TRONS ONLY." Then he reached down and cut the ignition. The air conditioning expired with a sigh.

"You'll see," he said. "You'll wake up one morning ten years from now with a job and a wife and you'll say to yourself, oh yeah, I didn't realize it at the time, but that's when I was really happy."

The funeral director, Mr. Woodley, was tall, well-dressed, and extremely formal. He reminded me of a butler in an old movie. Bob and I followed him to the end of a dark corridor where the two other pallbearers were waiting, leaning against a wall on either side of a water fountain.

"Robert and Buddy," Mr. Woodley said, "I'd like you to meet Al and Bernie, colleagues of the deceased from the New Jersey Freight Company, Incorporated. Al and Bernie, please meet Robert and Buddy. Robert is married to the stepdaughter of the deceased. Buddy was his next-door neighbor for many years."

The four of us shook hands like football captains meeting for the coin toss. Bernie was a wild-looking guy with porkchop sideburns and a Roy Orbison haircut. Al was barely five feet tall but he had the chest and shoulders of a weightlifter. Neither of them looked comfortable in their suits.

After the brief service, a young guy, not much older than me, wheeled the closed casket into the hallway on a metal table. He had shaggy blond hair and an impressive tan. It was easy to imagine him in a wetsuit, with a surfboard tucked under one arm. I wondered how he'd ended up working in a funeral home.

Mr. Woodley arranged us symmetrically around the polished wooden box. "Gentlemen," he said, "because there is no formal church service today, our task is extremely simple. We have to transport the deceased from the door to the hearse. That is all. Once we arrive at the cemetery, their people will take over."

We walked in formation beside the coffin as

the assistant guided it slowly down the hallway. Bob and I were stationed in front. Mr. Woodley went ahead of us and opened the wide double doors at the end of the hallway. Sunlight flooded in over his dark silhouette. We paused momentarily at the threshold for the assistant to come around to the front of the coffin. The mourners were gathered on the lawn, watching us. Beyond them, at the curb, the hearse waited, its back gate swung open.

"Gentlemen, please grasp the handles. On the count of three, will you please lift." The handle was a grooved brass rod hinged to the side of the box. It fit nicely in my hand.

"One . . . two . . . three."

The casket lifted easily off the gurney, almost as though it were empty, but then the weight shifted and we had to struggle for a moment to get it stabilized. It struck me suddenly—I had somehow managed not to think of it until then—that Mr. Norman's dead body was inside the box. I glanced over at Bob. He looked shaken; a drop of sweat slid like a tear down the side of his face. I was glad he had Al backing him up.

We took our first tentative step forward, out into the air. It was a warm, hazy day with a sweet breeze blowing. Birds and squirrels chattered in the trees around the funeral home.

"Gentlemen, please watch your step as we descend the stairs."

I took the instruction literally, staring at my new loafers as we moved toward the sidewalk, one cement step at a time. I could hear the assistant grunting as he helped us support the front end, where all the weight was concentrated.

It felt like we were moving in slow motion as we passed the mourners. I heard a sniffle and looked up. Mrs. Norman was standing on the grass, her face concealed by a gauzy black veil. I felt a jolt when our eyes met.

There were metal rollers on the inside bed of the hearse. The coffin slid in easily and thudded against the back wall. I imagined Mr. Norman wincing at the impact.

"Thank God that's over with," Bob whispered as we walked across the lawn to join the other mourners.

About twenty people had attended the funeral, but only seven showed up for lunch afterwards at the Normans'. Besides the immediate family and the pallbearers, the only other guest was Estelle, a skinny, middle-aged woman who lived down the street and spent a lot of time sitting on her front porch in a rocking chair. At the cemetery she cried so hard that Mrs. Norman had to stroke her hair to get her to calm down.

There was a catered buffet of cold cuts and Italian food set up on the kitchen table. I filled my paper plate and headed out to the patio. The women stayed inside, so it was just the four pall-bearers gathered around the picnic table Mr. Norman had assembled a few years ago from a kit. I remembered coming up the driveway one day and seeing the pieces of the table scattered on the lawn. It took him a whole weekend to put it together.

Al raised his beer bottle. "Here's to Jerry. He'll be missed."

We clinked bottles and drank to Mr. Norman. Bernie unknotted his tie. "Man," he said, "that coffin was heavier than it looked." He yanked the tie free from his collar and stuffed it in his coat pocket. "It felt like a goddam refrigerator."

For the first time all day, Bob grinned. Sweat stains had soaked all the way through his dark suit. He looked like a basketball coach whose team had just won in overtime. "No kidding," he said. "I wasn't sure if we were going to make it down those stairs."

We ate without speaking. The food was wonderful, and I felt unreasonably hungry, like I hadn't eaten for days. I finished a turkey sandwich and was halfway through a serving of lasagna when Estelle came out and told us that Millie had something to show us in the living room.

"Something about Jerry," she added nervously. She was standing at the edge of the patio wearing a big pink oven mitt on one hand. When she saw that we weren't getting up right away, she pulled a lawn chair up to the table and sat down.

"I live alone," she announced. "I don't have a car. It's not easy for me to get around." She spoke quickly, as if pressed for time, her words tumbling out one on top of the other. Her eyes were moist and slightly distorted behind thick glasses. "Whenever I needed to go somewhere I called Jerry and he said, 'Estelle, I'll be right over.'" She tried to smile but her lips began quivering. She buried her face in the oven mitt.

All the curtains were drawn in the living room. We had to bring in extra chairs from the kitchen to get everyone seated. Judy, Mrs. Norman, and Estelle were squeezed together on the couch. There was a carousel slide projector set up on the coffee table.

Judy stood up. She kept her head down and her hands folded as she spoke. "My mother would like to thank you all for joining us in this difficult hour. She thought you might like to see Jerry one last time before you go." Mrs. Norman nodded, and even in the dim light you could see that her face was swollen and blurred with grief. Judy sat down and switched on the projector. It was squat and round, like a miniature flying saucer. A fan started humming and a blank square of light appeared on the wall. She clicked the advance button three or four times before the first fuzzy image filled the empty space. Mrs. Norman adjusted the lens, and her husband jumped into focus. He was walking through the front door, carrying groceries into the house. He seemed happy to be home.

I glanced at Bob. He was sitting next to me, pressing his fist against his mouth, biting down hard on the thumb. Dozens of pictures flashed and vanished on the wall. Most of them were candid shots taken around the house. Mr. Norman stood by the bathroom sink, smiling through a beard of shaving cream. He mowed the lawn in a sleeveless T-shirt. He sat in a chair looking gloomy.

Mr. Norman took out the garbage. He did a wild dance at Judy's wedding, waving a napkin over his head. In Atlantic City, he hit the jackpot on a slot machine; coins poured like water into his plastic cup. Mr. Norman read a magazine. He gave Halloween candy to a child dressed as a ghost. He sat with me on the couch.

For some reason, Judy let that image linger. In the photograph, I had long curly hair and wore a blue flannel shirt. I couldn't believe how young and fragile I looked. Mr. Norman was huge in comparison. He had one arm around my shoulder, pulling me against him. Our eyes glowed red from the flash. Bob found my hand and squeezed it.

"That's you," he said, his startled voice breaking the silence in the living room.